Chartered Banker

GW00703397

PRACTICE & REVISION KIT
Operations Management

In this 2016/17 edition

- A **user-friendly format** for easy navigation
- **Updated** on recent developments
- **Question practice on each chapter** to test knowledge retention
- **Exam-standard** practice examinations

Chartered Banker
Leading financial professionalism

LEARNING MEDIA

Published August 2016

ISBN 9781 5097 0582 5

British Library Cataloguing-in-Publication Data
A catalogue record for this book
is available from the British Library

Published by
BPP Learning Media Ltd
BPP House, Aldine Place
London W12 8AA

www.bpp.com/learningmedia

Printed in United Kingdom by
RICOH UK Limited
Unit 2, Wells Place
Merstham RH1 3LG

Your learning materials, published by BPP Learning Media
Ltd, are printed on paper obtained from traceable
sustainable sources.

BPP
LEARNING MEDIA

CONTENTS

	Page	
	Questions	**Answers**

QUESTION BANK

Chapter 1 – The Banking Environment

Written Questions

Question 1

Explain the main triggers that led to the development of asset bubbles and the search for yield, in the global economy, in the period before the financial crisis.   **(5 marks)**

Question 2

Basel III was introduced in 2010 and updated the earlier Basel II Accords. What new regulations did it introduce?   **(5 marks)**

Question 3

Describe the pre-crisis regulatory regime and explain the roles of the then, regulators.   **(5 marks)**

Question 4

What are the main principles of the UK's Corporate Governance Code?   **(15 marks)**

Multiple Choice Questions

1   Why did securitisation become popular in the pre-crisis banking environment?

   A   It was a cheaper way for banks to increase liquidity and to raise funds for new lending

   B   It enabled banks to create Collateral Debt Obligations (CDOs) as a means of financing their balance sheets

   C   It allowed the banks to employ an 'originate and hold' funding model

   D   It improved the bank's credit ratings

2   Risk based capital is used for what?

   A   As a measure to monitor market risk

   B   To increase leverage and liquidity for UK banks

   C   To enforce good corporate governance on financial services organisations

   D   To set capital requirements for the size and degree of risks taken by an organisation

3   Which of the Basel accords introduced the concept of three pillars?

   A   Basel I

   B   Basel II

   C   Basel III

   D   All of the above

4   The OECD's principles defines corporate governance as

A   A set of relationships between a company's management, its board, shareholders and other stakeholders

B   A way of rebuilding trust and stability in the culture of banks and financial services organisations

C   A way for financial services organisations to develop sound control structures and strategies

D   A way to promote the success of an organisation by directing and supervising its responsibilities

5   The Higgs Report 2003 was established to review the effectiveness of

A   Corporate governance

B   The Chief Executive Officer

C   Directors and shareholders

D   Non executive directors

6   Which independent regulator has responsibility for corporate governance and reporting?

A   PRA

B   FCA

C   FRC

D   FPC

7   Value at Risk (VAR) has been described as a

A   Mathematical formulae used to measure risk of loss on financial assets

B   More robust way of modelling risk during market collapse, chaos or duress

C   Way measuring and maintaining 'tail-end' risk

D   Way to move quantitative risk to a more qualitative risk metric based on expected shortfalls

8   The first Basel Accord required banks to hold minimum levels of capital to what percentage of risk weighted assets?

A   2.5%

B   4.5%

C   7%

D   8%

9   Under section 173 of the Companies Act 2006 all directors of limited companies are required to

A   Exercise independent judgment

B   Set remuneration policy for the executive board

C   Set the risk management policies of the organisation

D   Protect their shareholders and employees

10 **The UK Corporate Governance Code requires the collective responsibility of the board to**

A Encourage dialogue with shareholders based on mutual understanding of objectives

B Arrange the Annual General Meeting (AGM)

C Demonstrate good corporate social responsibility (CSR)

D Offer sufficient remuneration to attract, retain and motivate executive employees and shareholders

11 **The Cadbury Report (1992) was concerned with**

A Corporate governance

B Banks becoming 'too big to fail'

C Financial stability of the UK's banking system

D Leveraging market discipline to encourage and motivate prudential management in UK banks

12 **The Basel II Accord required banks to engage in dialogue about their internal processes for measuring and managing risk. With whom do they do this?**

A Its regulators

B Its shareholders

C Its directors

D Its stakeholders

13 **Under Basel II the formulation of the internal capital adequacy assessment process was the duty and responsibility of whom?**

A The regulators

B The Prudential Regulation Authority

C The organisation's board of directors and senior management

D The credit rating agencies

14 **Securitised financing can be considered attractive because**

A Risks may be transferred and liabilities taken off balance sheet to free up a bank to write more business

B Loan to values usually increase when property prices are stable or increasing

C It improves a bank's standing and therefore its credit ratings

D Risk is more transparent and regulated

15 **Before the financial crisis, complexity and opacity of the global financial system grew, which meant**

A Problems or concerns in one part of the system could rapidly be transferred to another part of the system again and again

B The wholesale funding markets could expand expediently

C Risk became more quantifiable and manageable

D Financial disintermediation allowed investors to access funds from the bond markets thereby increasing the need to use banks as financial intermediaries

Chapter 2 – Bank Failures: Case Studies

Written Questions

Question 1

Briefly identify the key factors in the failure of RBS.

(15 marks)

Question 2

Briefly identify the key factors in the failure of HBOS.

(15 marks)

Multiple Choice Questions

1   What is meant by the term liquidity?

A   A measure of profitability

B   A measure of the extent that an organisation's assets cover the organisation's external liabilities

C   A measure of an organisation's ability to generate sufficient profits to meet its lending obligations in both the long and the short term

D   A measure of the extent to which an organisation has sufficient cash to meet its immediate and short term obligations when they fall due

2   Asset Backed Commercial Paper (ABCP) is

A   A type of commercial paper for which other financial assets stand as collateral

B   A type of bond that contains assets that back the interest and principal repayment of CDO conduits

C   A combination of cash and derivative instruments designed to secure the performance of another type of financial instrument

D   A type of indemnity secured by Treasury bills used in the Bank of England's Emergency Liquidity Assistance (ELA) scheme

3   The Special Resolution Regime (SRR)

A   Gave substantial powers to the tripartite regulators to deal with and stabilise banks that are in financial difficulties

B   Is the long term bail-out method used for banks and other financial service organisations who find themselves insolvent

C   Is the resolution fund used by central banks to finance the restructuring of failed credit institutions

D   Is the regime used to ring fence a retail bank's network to avoid banks being 'too big to fail'

4 **The Emergency Liquidity Assistance (ELA) scheme is**

A   The compensation fund of last resort for customers of authorised financial services organisations

B   A short term liquidity programme provided by central banks

C   The bail-out method used for banks and financial organisations who find themselves insolvent

D   A central bank initiative to provide asset cover for loan write-downs or write-offs

5 **Asset Backed Securities (ABS) are**

A   Bank of England special deposits

B   Legally binding contracts whose value is derived from another security

C   A financial security that is collateralised by assets such as bonds, loan repayments, leases or property

D   A form of collateralised debt obligation that invests in credit default swaps or other non cash assets held in a fixed term investment

6 **Liquidity Coverage Ratio (LCR) requires banks to have sufficient high quality liquid investments to withstand a stressed funding scenario, over what time period?**

A   Overnight

B   2 days

C   30 days

D   90 days

7 **A mono-line is**

A   A risk management product offered by export credit agencies to organisations wanting to protect themselves against loss of default, insolvency and bankruptcy

B   Where a company provides insurance or guarantee against the risk that a bond or other security will default

C   A combination of cash and derivative products designed to secure the performance of another financial entity

D   The method by which banks securitise their mortgage loan books to sell them to other institutions and investors for cash to increase liquidity

8 **Residential Mortgage Backed Securities (RMBS) are**

A   When borrowers with poor credit have higher rates placed on their mortgages to offset the increased risk of default

B   A combination of cash and derivative products designed to secure the performance of another financial instrument

C   A type of mortgage backed debt obligation whose cash flows come from a pool of mortgage related loans

D   Packaged residential mortgages held on a 'hold and originate' basis designed to raise additional liquidity

9   The Sterling Stock Regime (SSR) required banks to have sufficient high quality liquid assets to withstand a stressed funding scenario, over what time period?

A   Overnight

B   2 days

C   30 days

D   90 days

10   According to the House of Commons Treasury Committee (2009) Banking Crisis, the Governor of the Bank of England said that the most important common feature which distinguished the failed banks from the survivor banks was

A   Hubris

B   Leverage

C   Liquidity

D   Lack of capital

Chapter 3 – Post Crisis Regulation

Written Questions

Question 1

List the powers granted to the Financial Conduct Authority.   **(10 marks)**

Question 2

The Turner Review was commissioned to look at the events that led to the financial crisis and to recommend reforms. Detail its main findings.   **(15 marks)**

Question 3

According to the Treasury Select Committee, what were the origins of the banking crisis?   **(5 marks)**

Multiple Choice Questions

1   The Financial Services (Banking Reform) Bill, introduced in 2013, focussed on

A   Banks that were 'too big too fail'

B   Deregulating the financial services sector

C   Restoring trust in the banks and the UK's financial services sector

D   Changing the structure and delivery of regulation within the financial services

2   What is the Bank of England committed to do?

A   Imposing penalties for market abuse

B   Imposing banking capital and liquidity regulations

C   Promoting and maintaining monetary and financial stability

D   Increasing reporting requirements for financial institutions in the shadow banking sector

3   The Bank of England reports to Parliament through the

A   Treasury Select Committee

B   Chancellor of the Exchequer

C   First Lord of the Treasury

D   Financial Policy Committee

4   The Financial Policy Committee is charged with

A   Ensuring banking customers get a fair deal

B   Maintaining the efficiency of the financial system, both at home and abroad

C   Identifying, monitoring and removing systemic risk within the banking system

D   Regulation and supervision of banks, building societies, credit unions, insurers and major investment firms

5 **The Financial Policy Committee is able to make recommendations and give direction to**

A   FSA and FSB

B   PRA and FCA

C   FOS and FCA

D   FSB and PRA

6 **The Prudential Regulation Authority is responsible for**

A   Ensuring markets work well

B   The regulation and supervision of banks

C   Supporting the economic policy of the government

D   Approving persons in the financial services sector who have 'controlled function' roles

7 **The Financial Conduct Authority is responsible for ensuring**

A   Credit rating agencies are regulated

B   Markets work well so that consumers get a good deal

C   UK retail banks are 'ring fenced' from their investment banking arms

D   Consumer complaints against the bank are dealt with properly and can require them to pay compensation

8 **What was the Vickers Report was asked to consider?**

A   Identifying and managing macro-level systemic risk

B   Improving the risk management policies and frameworks in UK banks

C   Remuneration policies and practices that do not encourage or reward excessive risk taking

D   Structural and non structural reforms to the UK banking sector to promote financial stability and competition

9 **Basel III introduced the Net Stable Funding Ratio (NSFR). What is it?**

A   A capital directive to improve the quality and quantum of banks capital

B   A requirement that banks have sufficient high quality liquid assets to withstand a short term stressed scenario

C   A long term structural ratio designed to address liquidity mismatches

D   Strengthening the capital requirements for a bank's trading book to better reflect potential losses from adverse market movements

10 **'Wrong way' risk arises when**

A   Corporate governance is compromised

B   The quantum of risk 'balloons' at the end

C   Default risk and credit exposure increase together

D   Directive, preventative and corrective management controls fail

Chapter 4 – Corporate Social Responsibility and Sustainability

Written Questions

Question 1

What are the five sustainability considerations that are relevant to operational management?

(10 marks)

Question 2

What is the CB: PSB and what does it do? **(5 marks)**

Question 3

CSR and sustainability initiatives will affect many aspects of a business's operations. What five aspects would they include? **(15 marks)**

Multiple Choice Questions

1   **The ability of financial markets to keep going is based on**

A   Confidence

B   Investment

C   Social responsibility

D   Monetary policy

2   **Corporate social responsibility is a form of**

A   Ethics

B   Corporate sustainability

C   Corporate governance

D   Corporate self-regulation integrated into a business model

3   **CSR can be described as**

A   Moral principles that promote ethical competence in the way a business behaves

B   A code of corporate governance principles embedded into a businesses mission statement

C   An obligation, beyond that required by the law, for a business to pursue long term goals that are good for society

D   Business operations that are not harmful to the environment or depleting natural resources, thereby supporting long-term ecological balance

4   The Banking Standards Board (BSB) was established to

A   Promote higher standards of lending practices as detailed in the Lending Code

B   Promote high standards of ethical behaviour and competence across the banking sector

C   Promote a forward looking approach to capital supervision and risk management

D   Improve standards and prudential conduct for the financial services sector throughout the UK

5   In terms of product governance, delivering the right outcome for customers is critical and that means replacing the 'product push' approach of the past with a

A   Product push/pull approach

B   Product life cycle approach

C   Omni-channel approach

D   Data-analytical marketing approach

6   A socially responsible organisation should be

A   An ethical organisation

B   A sustainable organisation

C   A well governed organisation

D   An ecologically responsible organisation

7   CSR is about responsibility to all

A   Owners

B   Employees

C   Stakeholders

D   Shareholders

8   Which governmental initiative provides a State guarantee to customers of a failed financial institution?

A   FCA

B   MAS

C   FSCS

D   EFGS

9   Ethics is all about?

A   CSR

B   Being good

C   Corporate governance

D   Morally correct behaviour

10   Large organisations can show some social responsibility by

A   Reducing consumer costs

B   Increasing employment

C   Making charitable donations

D   Using local suppliers where possible

Chapter 5 – Banking Operational Models and Service Quality

Written Questions

Question 1

What are the characteristics of mission statements and what criteria are used to judge the effectiveness of a corporate mission statement? **(10 marks)**

Question 2

How can mission statements play an important role in the strategic planning process? **(10 marks)**

Question 3

In the context of service quality, what are the five key gaps frequently referred to for helping to identify the gaps between the perceived service quality that customers receive and their expectations? **(10 marks)**

Multiple Choice Questions

1 **The Ashridge Mission model of mission statements links business strategy to**

A   Wealth creation

B   Culture and ethics

C   Competitive advantage

D   Standards of behaviour

2 **What is horizontal integration?**

A   Using current capabilities by developing activities that are competitive with or directly complementary to its present activities

B   A strategy whose goal is to synchronise information technology (IT) and business cultures and objectives to align technology with strategy and goals

C   The combination and transformation of independent components of business organisations into cohesive and synergistic entities

D   It involves focusing on the capabilities that would improve speed, quality and efficiency and pruning business activities that no longer fit the value-creation logic of the corporate strategy

3 **What is vertical integration?**

A   Where a strategy to grow market share or profits through product and service innovation

B   When a company expands backwards or forwards within its existing value network and therefore becomes its own supplier or distributor

C   A product penetration strategy where a company introduces existing products into new geographical markets

D   A growth strategy designed to encourage advancements in technology or services by investing in research and development activities

4   Analytics are designed to

A   Produce intelligence, not information

B   Capture, curate and aggregate large amounts of business data

C   Create a distributed file sharing framework for data storage and interrogation

D   Find the right balance between IT infrastructure and innovation to maximise business value

5   Service quality can be defined as

A   Having the best products in the market place

B   Making sure the customer comes back to purchase more

C   Satisfying customers needs before, during and after the sale

D   Meeting or exceeding customers' expectations at a price that is acceptable to the customer and at a return that is acceptable to the organisation

6   Service quality gaps can emerge because of

A   Poor pricing

B   Misunderstanding, misinterpretation or mismanagement

C   Inadequate training where staff are not fully aligned or focused in a way that puts the customer first

D   Product push strategies where reward and compensation are deemed to be more important than treating customers nicely

7   The essence of good customer service is that the

A   Product benefits actually occur

B   Buyer and supplier develop a mutually beneficial relationship

C   Products produced are cheaper and solve a problem more effectively than the products or services offered by rivals

D   Products are produced at the right time, in the right place, and at the right price for the customer

8   A service level agreement (SLA) is

A   Part of a service contract where the level of service is clearly defined

B   A non-negotiable agreement between the customer and the supplier

C   A legally binding contract of competence between suppliers and purchasers

D   A mutually binding contract of competence between suppliers and purchasers

9   Studies show that a percentage of customers who defected to competitors had scored themselves as being 'satisfied' or 'very satisfied' in customer satisfaction surveys. What is the level?

A   42%

B   63%

C   80%

D   100%

10 **Customer satisfaction is a passive state, whereas customer loyalty is**

A   The positive intention to stay

B   The best way to get new business

C   Where the customer becomes immune to all competitor approaches

D   Where the business adds more value and at a lower cost than competitor rivals

Chapter 6 – Operational Risk Management

Written Questions

Question 1

Explain the 'three lines of defence' model used in risk management.   **(10 marks)**

Question 2

Describe the operational risk event types as outlined by the Basel Accords that are applicable in the banking industry.   **(8 marks)**

Question 3

What are the benefits of operational risk management in banking?   **(5 marks)**

Question 4

Name the different benefits that can spin off from the actual activities of operational risk management.   **(5 marks)**

Question 5

What should the risk policy of any organisation should aim to do?   **(5 marks)**

Multiple Choice Questions

1   How often must a bank report to the FCA on complaints received?
- A   Annually
- B   Six-monthly
- C   Monthly
- D   Never

2   The Basel Committee on Banking Supervision defines operational risk as:
- A   The risk of loss due to inadequacies in capital, supervision or market discipline
- B   The risk of loss resulting from inadequate or failed internal processes, people and systems or from external events
- C   Managing the exposure to the frequency and severity of expected losses as well as unexpected losses
- D   A probability or threat of damage, injury, liability, or any other negative occurrence that is caused by external or internal vulnerabilities

3 In managing operational risk the establishment of the risk control framework and the corporate governance measures under which it operates lies with the

A Board

B Directors

C Shareholders

D Stakeholders

4 Who is accountable to the Executive Committee and the Board for enabling the business to balance risk and reward?

A The directors

B The chief risk officer

C The audit committee

D The external auditors

5 The purpose of audit is to

A Balance the books

B Sample the financial records

C Provide an independent review

D Provide a true and fair view of the financial statements

6 External audit operates for the purpose of reporting to the

A Directors

B Stakeholders

C Chief risk officer

D Members and shareholders of a company

7 Which regulatory body's rules state that, 'a firm should ensure that all employees are aware of their responsibility and role in operational risk management and are suitable and capable of performing these responsibilities?'

A FPC

B PRA

C FCA

D Basel

Chapter 7 – Operational Management

Written Questions

Question 1

[handwritten: high strategic risk, low vulnerabilities, low risk more flexible / transaction costs / core competences with ongoing competitive advantage]

Describe the three tests to establish whether an activity should be outsourced. **(5 marks)**

Question 2

[handwritten: Reacting Anticipating Collaborating Orchestrating]

A demand network is the result of companies evolving internally or within their departments and externally with their partners. This evolution is a four-stage process. What are the stages? **(5 marks)**

Question 3

[handwritten: Network Rather than a Pipeline]

What is the aim of an integrated supply chain model? **(10 marks)**

[handwritten: COORDINATE WHOLE CHAIN → Integrate: from Raw Material supplies to end Customer]

Multiple Choice Questions

1 The overall objective of operations is to

A Produce goods and services

B Manage and maintain quality

C Manage resources effectively and efficiently

D Use a transformation process to add value and create competitive advantage

2 The value a business adds arises from a collection of outcomes, not from

A Effective pricing

B Lean production

C Supply and demand

D Activities and processes

3 According to Porter's analysis of the value chain, business activities are not the same as

A Primary activities

B Secondary activities

C Business functions

D Support functions

4 Porter distinguished between primary activities and support activities. Primary activities are those directly related with

A Purchasing and procurement

B The costs of carrying out value activities

C Production, sales, marketing, delivery and services

D Human resources, technology and infrastructural functions

5   Process mapping aims to

A   Cut costs

B   Identify the 'one best way'

C   Build supply chains in response to demand signals

D   Identify and represent the steps and decisions involved in a process

6   What does operational management tries to ensure?

A   Integration of the value chain

B   Value creation for shareholders

C   Costs are reduced and production maximised

D   Organisations are run as efficiently as possible

7   Translating business or market strategy into an operations strategy requires identifying what?

A   Risk

B   Value creation

C   Competitive factors

D   Return on capital employed

8   Strategies should be continually reviewed in response to what?

A   Cash flows

B   Consumer demand

C   Changes in the environment

D   Shareholder/investor requirements

9   Kotler wrote of meeting customer requirements as 'identifying value, delivering value', and what else?

A   Sharing value

B   Creating value

C   Managing value

D   Communicating value

10   Porter's value chain is a model of

A   Value activities

B   Product differentiation

C   Cost leadership

D   Market attractiveness

Chapter 8 – Quality Management

Written Questions

Question 1 — TQM

The mnemonic PRECEPT is used to understand the key elements of TQM. What does it stand for and what does each letter mean? **(5 marks)**

Question 2

Lean production or lean process improvement involves the systematic elimination of waste. Provide examples of waste. **(5 marks)**

— Lean Prod

Question 3

What are the benefits of adopting lean production techniques? **(10 marks)**

Question 4

What is SERVQUAL? Measuring Quality **(10 marks)**

Multiple Choice Questions

1   Quality is concerned with

A   Kanban

B   Zero waste

C   Fitness for purpose

D   Cost management

2   Quality management is concerned with

A   Controls

B   Inspection

C   Ensuring that products or services meet their planned level of quality and conform to specifications

D   Straight through processing to reduce the amount of human input required to process transactions

3   Modern approaches to quality focus on

A   Inspection

B   Cost controls

C   Waste management and human resources

D   The prevention of defects through quality standards and processes

4 **The balanced scorecard focuses on a number of different perspectives. How many?**

A 2

B 4

C 6

D 8

5 **Continuous improvement is sometimes referred to as**

A TQM

B Kaizen

C Kanban

D Six Sigma

6 **Six Sigma is a process designed to help organisations to focus on**

A Lean production

B Plan Do Check Act (PDCA) to deliver continuous improvement

C Developing and delivering near-perfect products and services

D Elimination of waste in terms of time and resources used in production

7 **Lean production involves**

A Identifying and eliminating all non value-adding activities

B Developing inventory control systems to control the supply chain

C Integrating operational processes to smooth out production flows

D Enhancing the customer value chain to exceed their expectations

8 **Discipline, simplicity, pride, standardisation and repeatability are emphasised as being critical to efficiency in which model?**

A The 5Ss

B The 5 Whys

C The 5Vs

D Six Sigma

9 **What is a key feature of 'world class' manufacturing?**

A Six Sigma

B Process mapping

C Flexibility of production

D Customer engagement and satisfaction

10 **Quality control is concerned with**

A Process mapping

B Flexibility of production

C Customer engagement and satisfaction

D Checking and reviewing work that has been done

Chapter 9 – Quality Management Techniques

Written Questions

Question 1

What does visual management help to do? *(handwritten)* (5 marks)

Question 2

Explain what standard operating procedures (SOPs) are and what they do. *(handwritten: SOPs)* (5 marks)

Question 3

What are the benefits of using standard operating procedures (SOPs)? *(handwritten: SOPs)* (5 marks)

Question 4

A problem is something that presents itself as a barrier to an organisation and can relate to the way the work is designed or done. How are problems defined and how can they arise? (10 marks)

(handwritten: P&Cs)

Multiple Choice Questions

1   Lean defines a problem as

A   A gap to a standard

B   Something to be worked out or solved

C   Any question raised for inquiry, consideration, or solution

D   Any question or matter involving doubt, uncertainty, or difficulty

2   P&Cs ensure that

A   There are no deviations from standard

B   Planning and control systems are all fit for purpose

C   Customer complaints are eradicated

D   Problems and issues are identified, understood and managed consistently

3   A tally sheet is used to

A   Identify counter measures in problem resolution

B   Ensure consistency and visibility across the whole organisation

C   Gather data to help in assessing the situation and to focus on the real issues

D   Promote sound management through the sharing of good practice

4 **Which is the best tool for identifying the work flows across several teams, departments or people?**

A   The 5 whys

B   Fish bone diagrams

C   Swim-lane process maps

D   Plan Do Check Act (PDCA)

5 **Brainstorming allows the team to**

A   Generate ideas and boost creativity

B   Systematically identify and understand problems

C   Develop a model to plan changes aimed at improvement

D   Structure and categorise previously unknown relationships

6 **The priority matrix is based on**

A   Urgency and importance

B   Number and size of impacts

C   Time and costs involved to reach a solution

D   Ease of implementation and the size of the impact

7 **Validating is which part of the PDCA cycle?**

A   Plan

B   Do

C   Check

D   Act

8 **In terms of standard operating procedures (SOP) what does standardisation mean?**

A   The process of implementing and developing technical standards

B   Making things of the same type so all have the same basic features

C   Finding the one best way of doing things and getting everyone to do it that way

D   The process of creating, issuing and implementing standards across the entire organisation

9 **SWOT analysis seeks to turn threats into**

A   Strengths

B   Weaknesses

C   Opportunities

D   All of the above

10 **The PDCA cycle can be used as a model for**

A   Efficiency

B   Root cause analysis

C   Counter measures

D   Improvement activity

Chapter 10 – Management Accounting and Management Information

Written Questions

Question 1

Why are budgets useful? **(10 marks)**

Question 2

To be useful, information requires a number of specific qualities. The mnemonic ACCURATE is a useful way of remembering them. List the qualities and provide an example for each. **(10 marks)**

Question 3

What is the Lending Code and what products does it cover? **(10 marks)**

Multiple Choice Questions

1   Financial accounting is concerned with

   A   Strategy

   B   Stewardship

   C   Certifying value

   D   Balancing the books

2   Management accounting differs from financial accounting because it emphasises

   A   Cost containment

   B   Purpose rather than techniques

   C   Income, assets, liabilities and cash flow

   D   The future direction the business is taking

3   A budget is

   A   Based on accurate, empirical evidence of performance

   B   Used to provide a 'true and fair view' of the financial statements

   C   A plan of revenues and expenses that the organisation expects for a forthcoming period

   D   A working document of all cash transactions on which cost schedules and variance reporting can be based

4   Environmental scanning is

A   Understanding the life cycles of both markets and products

B   The process of gathering external information from a wide range of sources

C   Monitoring the financial markets in which a company operates

D   Using market strategy based on either cost leadership, differentiation or a combination of both

5   Transaction processing systems (TPS) are used

A   By management to assist in making decisions on issues which are subject to high levels of uncertainty

B   For routine tasks in which data items or transactions must be processed so that operations can continue

C   To facilitate the creation and integration of new knowledge into an organisation

D   By pooling data from internal and external sources and makes information available to senior managers in an easy-to-use form

6   Executive information systems (EIS) are used

A   By management to assist in making decisions on issues which are subject to high levels of uncertainty

B   For routine tasks in which data items or transactions must be processed so that operations can continue

C   To facilitate the creation and integration of new knowledge into an organisation

D   By pooling data from internal and external sources and makes information available to senior managers in an easy-to-use form

7   Decision support systems (DSS) are used

A   By management to assist in making decisions on issues which are subject to high levels of uncertainty

B   For routine tasks in which data items or transactions must be processed so that operations can continue

C   To facilitate the creation and integration of new knowledge into an organisation

D   By pooling data from internal and external sources and makes information available to senior managers in an easy-to-use form

8   Knowledge work systems (KWS) are used

A   By management to assist in making decisions on issues which are subject to high levels of uncertainty

B   For routine tasks in which data items or transactions must be processed so that operations can continue

C   To facilitate the creation and integration of new knowledge into an organisation

D   By pooling data from internal and external sources and makes information available to senior managers in an easy-to-use form

9 **Office automation systems (OAS) are**

A   Internal information structures used in the aggregation of Big Data

B   Management information systems that convert data into summary reports

C   Computer systems designed to increase the productivity of data and information workers

D   Computerised management accounting schedules designed to provide senior management with real time performance data

10 **Compliance with the terms of the Lending Code is independently monitored and enforced by which body?**

A   The Financial Conduct Authority

B   The Lending Standards Board

C   The Consumer Credit Council

D   The British Bankers Association

Chapter 11 – Capacity Management

Written Questions

Question 1

Capacity planning in the short and medium-term has several implications for operational performance. Describe them. **(10 marks)**

Question 2

Explain what Materials Requirements Planning (MRP I) is and what benefits it provides. **(10 marks)**

Question 3

Explain what Manufacturing Resource Planning (MRP II) is and what benefits it can provide. **(10 marks)**

Multiple Choice Questions

1   Capacity management aims to

A   Minimise waste by using push or pull controls to manage work flows

B   Minimise inventory levels by adopting lean manufacturing techniques

C   Maximise workflows during times of predictable and unpredictable demand

D   Maximise the returns an organisation achieves on the assets and systems it uses

2   Overcapacity means resources available for production are

A   Fully utilised

B   Not fully utilised

C   Fully utilised in response to predictable demand

D   Not fully utilised in response to unpredictable demand

3   Dependent demand relates to demand that is

A   Predictable because it is based on factors that are known

B   Predictable because it is based on factors that are unknown

C   Unpredictable because it is based on factors that are known

D   Unpredictable because it is based on factors that are unknown

4   The objective of capacity planning is to

A   Reduce costs

B   Minimise inventory levels

C   Maximise both profits and customer satisfaction

D   Minimise lead times throughout the supply chain

5   Kanban is a form of

A   Push control

B   Pull control

C   Loading control

D   Sequencing control

6   With 'pull' control, there should be

A   Less inventory in the system

B   More inventory in the system

C   More capacity in the system

D   Less capacity in the system

7   A level capacity plan is aimed at

A   Reducing inventory levels and obsolescence

B   Maximising profits and customer satisfaction

C   Planning inventory levels and lead times throughout the entire supply chain

D   Maintaining activity at a constant level over a period ignoring fluctuations in forecast demand

8   Chase demand aims to

A   Reduce inventory levels and obsolescence

B   Match capacity to forecast fluctuations in demand

C   Reduce peak demand by switching it to the off-peak periods

D   Balance customer waiting time and idle service capacity

9   Capacity management may be measured in terms of

A   Bottlenecks

B   Queuing times

C   Return on capital employed

D   Input resources and outputs produced

10   Sequencing refers to

A   Forecasting demand

B   The amount of work allocated to an operating unit

C   The order that different jobs will be done or orders fulfilled

D   Scheduling a timetable specifying the time jobs will take

Chapter 12 – Banking Innovation

Written Questions

Question 1

Explain what cheque imaging is and what benefits will accrue for banks and their customers.**(10 marks)**

Question 2

What are the advantages and disadvantages of a centralised system or department?   **(8 marks)**

Question 3

What are the advantages and disadvantages of a decentralised system or department?   **(7 marks)**

Question 4

Big Data has a role to play in information management and can be defined by considering the three Vs. Explain what the 3Vs are.   **(5 marks)**

Multiple Choice Questions

1   In the cheque clearing cycle how soon do customers start to earn interest after depositing a cheque?

A   Day 1

B   Day 2

C   Day 4

D   Day 6

2   According to the British Bankers Association UK businesses have an overreliance on bank sourced credit. What level of credit did it suggest?

A   60%

B   70%

C   80%

D   90%

3   What is cited as the most expensive payment option for retailers?

A   Cash

B   Cheques

C   Credit cards

D   Charge cards

4   Big Data is being used in

A   The pursuit of value creation

B   The design of corporate strategy models

C   Peer to peer lending (P2P) and crowd funding

D   The Financial Ombudsman Services complaint management procedures

5   When did the first internet only bank first appear?

A   1980

B   1985

C   1990

D   1995

6   The payment services regulator seeks to

A   Speed up payment services

B   Regulate the banking industry

C   Arbitrate in payment services disputes

D   Promote competition and innovation in payment services

7   What are the shared service centres intended to improve?

A   Centralisation

B   Risk control and compliance

C   Improving back office efficiency

D   Staff welfare and production capability

8   Which functions are not, typically, decentralised?

A   Sales and marketing

B   Back office functions

C   Risk and compliance

D   Human resource management

9   On average, mobile banking consumers interact with their bank, more often than online banking. By how much?

A   3 times

B   20 times

C   60 times

D   About the same

10   Big Data analytics are used to analyse data in order to develop corporate strategy to improve, what?

A   Profitability

B   Technology

C   Customer trends

D   Systems and procedures

Chapter 13 – Digitalisation of the Banking Industry

Written Questions

Question 1

What are the barriers to the benefits of data analytics, in banking? **(15 marks)**

Question 2

What are the advantages of data analytics for both banks and their customers? **(15 marks)**

Multiple Choice Questions

1 Digitalisation of banks is transforming service delivery from a multichannel approach to

A A brand marketing approach

B An omni-channel approach

C A consumer lifecycle approach

D A micro-marketing segmentation approach

2 The European Banking Federation signed a Memorandum of Understanding with Europol in 2014 which allows for the

A Integration of capital markets

B Sharing of relevant information on cyber threats

C Coordination of a Digital Single Digital Market (DSM)

D Adoption of a single supervisory mechanism throughout the EU

3 The key to a successful Digital Single Market is

A Trust

B FinTechs

C Globalisation

D Integration of legacy systems

4 Distributed ledgers are commonly referred to as

A Blockchain

B FinTechs

C Management accounts

D Crypto-technologies

Handwritten annotations:

Data Analytics → Through the data obtained by banks & analysing them through effective analytical tools & algorithms they anticipate customer needs, without customers having to provide info, and this + tailor solutions accordingly.

→ Barriers to Benefits of Data Analytics

Customer
• Customer Experience
→ Timely → offers in real time
→ more informed
→ Conf. sharing data
→ High confidentiality
→ Tailored solutions
→ more efficient
→ with min effort from customer side
→ better outcome

Bank
• Understand what the customer needs
• Products & services to offer making them more trustworthy
• more efficient, cost effective
• edge over competitors
• Fraud prevention & creditworthiness

→ advantages of Data Analytics

Big Data / Blockchain / Cloud Computing Challenge
• Regulation regards Outsourcing - so Audit Risk
• Banks in Early Stage of Adoption of this technology.
• Where Banks are concerned
 → Security
 → Data Protection
 → Privacy
 → Malware
 → Data Breach

• Uncertainty our liability — these to be viewed

• Geolocation of an EU customer in EU market v.s. US can be tracked anywhere in the world

Data Ownership
• Who owns the Data - Responsible
• Where it originally from
• Who has archived

• No value in Big Data but in Data Analytics of the Bank which & how much time they take to collate & analyse & make sense of data & need based tech required to store

• lack of level Playing field?
• Costly also Where Pseudo Anonymous confidential data

• Lay standards and common data architecture to be shared gives all European Fin Services branches
• Ultimately the data of an user. He can ask it to be deleted & modify the data & processor.

5   The EBF 'Blueprint' focuses on challenges and opportunities in

A   FinTechs

B   Retail banking

C   Legacy systems

D   Data management

6   The EBF is committed to

A   Regulating the European banking system

B   The Digital Single Market

C   International currency payments system

D   All of the above

7   Banks core values are

1   Trust

2   Privacy

3   Security

4   Integrity

5   Shareholder value

Choose the correct option A,B,C or D

A   1, 2, and 3 only

B   1, 2, 3, and 4 only

C   1 and 5 only

D   2, 3, 4 and 5 only

8   Consumers born between 1977 and 1994 are commonly referred to as

A   Generation W

B   Generation X

C   Generation Y

D   Generation Z

9   Digitalisation creates new opportunities to engage with consumers

A   Differently

B   In real time

C   Productively

D   Throughout the European financial markets

10   In 2015 an internet security threat report said 60% of all targeted cyber attacks affected

A   Banks

B   SMEs

C   Retail banking systems

D   Computer legacy systems

Chapter 14 – Creativity and What the Future May Hold

Written Questions

Question 1

According to Professor Teresa Amabile, what are the three components of creativity and what managerial practices affect creativity the most? **(15 marks)**

Question 2

Futurists use a five stage analytical process to develop descriptions of possible futures. What are they? **(5 marks)**

Question 3

When scanning the horizon futurists use two types of scanning techniques. Describe them. **(5 marks)**

Most futurists get information from a wide variety of sources including newspapers, books, periodicals, scientific and trade journals, forecasts, interviews with subject matter experts, electronic media, arts and cultural trends.

While most futurists scan broadly for background information, it is most effective when used in combination with a defined, focused framework.

Multiple Choice Questions

1   If an organisation is committed to innovation, they need to have

A   Significant financial resources

B   A high tolerance for risk and failure

C   A culture of evaluation and extrinsic motivation

D   Competitive monetary rewards and compensation structures in place

2   An intrapreneur is

A   An entrepreneur within an already established organisation

B   A business owner who has considerable initiative and risk aversion

C   A lateral thinker with strong business acumen and enthusiasm for what they do best

D   A creative thinker who embodies skill, experience, knowledge and passion for the business they own

3   Innovation economics is an economic theory that emphasises

A   Entrepreneurship, intrapreneurship and innovation

B   Productivity and economic growth to deliver benefits to society

C   Diversified production structures that exploit synergies and therefore innovation

D   Capital accumulation and investment predominantly used in research and development

4   What are the two axes in the product life cycle model?

A   Products and markets

B   Sales volumes and time

C   Cost leadership and differentiation

D   Market attractiveness and competitive advantage

5   In the product life cycle, at which point does turnover/sales peak?

A   Introduction

B   Growth

C   Maturity

D   Decline

6   To be creative, an idea must be

A   Patented

B   Distinctive

C   Cost effective

D   Appropriate, useful and actionable

7   An example of extrinsic motivation would be

A   A business start up

B   The 'carrot or a stick' method of motivation

C   A passion and interest in doing what you choose to do

D   An entrepreneur who embodies skill, experience, knowledge and desire to succeed

8   Which of the following is not a function of creativity?

A   Expertise

B   Motivation

C   Resources

D   Creative thinking skills

9   A professional futurist is a person who studies the future in order to

A   Predict the future

B   Forecast upcoming events

C   Gain economic insight from data or models based on past and future behaviours

D   Help people understand, anticipate, prepare for and gain advantage from coming changes

10   An inventor produces

A   Risk

B   Ideas

C   Profits

D   Patented products

ANSWER BANK

Chapter 1 – The Banking Environment

Answer 1

Before the financial crisis there were a number of reasons why asset bubbles developed which in turn, led to the 'search for yield'.

- With real and nominal interest rates decreasing, investors sought riskier, higher yielding assets in order to maintain nominal returns.

- Falling interest rates reduced the discount rate for valuing assets, thereby pushing up their prices.

- Rising collateral values fuelled consumer spending and encouraged higher borrowing and indebtedness, especially to purchase property, resulting in a diminished perception of the risks of debt.

- It was increasingly assumed that low inflation would persist, so keeping interest rates and debt servicing costs down.

- Property prices across a range of countries rose rapidly during this period. Strong economic growth, low unemployment and rising property prices all contributed to a perception that lending to the housing market was very low risk over the longer term.

Answer 2

The new Basel III regulations included:

- Tighter definitions of common equity, with a requirement for banks to hold 4.5% by January 2015 (compared with 2.0% previously), then a further capital conservation buffer of 2.5% to withstand future periods of stress, totalling 7%.

- A framework for counter-cyclical capital buffers, with banks having a capital ratio below 2.5% facing restrictions on dividends, buybacks and bonuses.

- Measures to limit counterparty credit risk.

- Short and medium-term quantitative liquidity ratios.

- The introduction of an internationally harmonised leverage ratio, acting as a backstop to risk-based capital measures.

Answer 3

In 1997, the Government set out a new framework for financial services and financial stability. It brought together regulatory responsibility for all financial services under one body, the Financial Services Authority (FSA) and set up a tripartite regulatory framework where each authority had its own distinct remit:

- The FSA was responsible for prudential and conduct of business regulation of all financial services including banks and building societies.

- The Bank of England gained powers to set interest rates, independent of Government, but relinquished responsibility for banking supervision to the FSA. The Bank's core purpose remained to ensure monetary and financial stability and it retained a surveillance function, to identify threats to the financial system.

- The Treasury was responsible for the institutional structure of financial regulation and legislation and, in the event of a crisis, for authorising certain types of financial interventions and keeping Parliament informed.

The tripartite set out arrangements for dealing with a possible financial crisis. A Memorandum of Understanding (MoU) confirmed the Bank of England's responsibility for the stability of the financial system as a whole; the FSA's responsibilities for prudential and conduct of business supervision; and gave the Treasury a clearly defined locus of control in exceptional cases.

The Bank and FSA were responsible for alerting the Treasury to cases with potential system-wide consequences.

Answer 4

The UK's Corporate Governance Code was introduced in 1998. While the Code does not carry legal force, it is a requirement under the Listing Rules of the London Stock Exchange that all listed companies either **comply** with its recommendations or explain to the shareholders the reasons for non-compliance.

The main principles of the Code are set out in five sections:

1   Leadership
2   Effectiveness
3   Accountability
4   Remuneration
5   Relations with shareholders

Leadership

Every company should be led by an effective board, collectively responsible for the long-term success of the company. There should be clear division of responsibility between those responsible for the direction of the company (the board) and those responsible for day-to-day operations (the executive). No individual should have unfettered powers of decision.

The Code stresses that the role of the Chairman is to lead the board of directors and ensure its effectiveness. It also highlights the duty of non-executive directors in constructively challenging and helping to develop proposals on strategy.

Effectiveness

The board of directors and its standing committees should be made up of an appropriate number of persons with an appropriate balance of skills, experience, independence and knowledge to enable them to discharge their duties effectively.

The procedures for the appointment of new directors should be formal, rigorous and transparent. Directors should be prepared to commit sufficient time to the company. On joining the board, new directors should receive induction. They should also update their knowledge and skills on a regular basis. To discharge their duties effectively, directors should be supplied with timely and good quality information. The board should undertake a formal, rigorous evaluation of its performance, and that of its standing committees, on an annual basis.

Accountability

The board should present a balanced and understandable assessment of the company's position and prospects. This commitment relates to the information that the company provides to its shareholders and others. The board must decide the nature and extent of the significant risks it will take in pursuing its objectives. To this end, it must maintain appropriate risk management and internal control systems.

There should be formal and transparent arrangements for considering how the board will apply corporate reporting, risk management and internal control principles, and for maintaining an appropriate relationship with the external auditors.

Remuneration

Remuneration offered and paid to directors should be sufficient to attract, retain and motivate directors of the quality required to run the company successfully, but they should not be paid too much. A significant proportion of executive directors' remuneration should be performance related in order to align the long-term interests of the company with the recipient.

There should be a formal and transparent procedure for developing policy on remuneration and for setting the remuneration of individual directors. This implies that there should be a focus on individual performance rather than collective pay awards across the board. Consistent with best practices in human resources management generally, no individual should be able to decide his or her own remuneration.

Relations with shareholders

It is the collective responsibility of the board to encourage dialogue with shareholders based on mutual understanding of objectives. The board should use the Annual General Meeting to communicate with investors and encourage their participation.

Comply and explain versus comply or be punished

With the exception of the US, all OECD countries including the UK, have adopted corporate governance codes that work on the 'comply or explain' principle; whereas the US – Sarbanes-Oxley (SOX) governance code works on the basis of 'comply or be punished.'

Multiple Choice Answers

1	**A**	Securitisation became popular in the pre-crisis environment because it was cheaper way for banks to increase liquidity and raise new funds for lending
2	**D**	Risk based capital is used to set capital requirements for the size and scope of risks taken by an organisation
3	**B**	Basel II introduced the concept of three pillars
4	**A**	The OECD's principles defines corporate governance as a set of relationships between a company's management, its board, shareholders and other stakeholders
5	**D**	The Higgs Report reviewed the effectiveness of non-executive directors (NEDs)
6	**C**	The Financial Reporting Council has responsibility for corporate governance and reporting
7	**A**	Value at Risk is a mathematical formula used to measure the risk of loss on financial assets
8	**D**	Basel I required banks to hold a minimum of 8% of capital
9	**A**	Under s173 of the Companies Act all directors of limited companies are required to exercise judgement
10	**A**	The UK Corporate Governance Code requires the board to encourage dialogue with shareholders based on mutual understanding of objectives
11	**A**	The Cadbury Report was concerned with corporate governance
12	**A**	Basel II requires banks to discuss their internal processes for measuring and managing risk with its regulators
13	**C**	Under Basel II the formulation of the internal capital adequacy assessment process is the responsibility of the organisation's Board of Directors and senior management
14	**A**	Securitisation financing is attractive because it allows risks to be transferred and liabilities to be taken off the balance sheet. This allows the bank to write more business
15	**A**	Prior to the financial crisis, complexity and opacity of the global financial system grew which meant that problems and concerns in one part of the system could rapidly be transferred to another part of the system repeatedly

Chapter 2 – Bank Failures: Case Studies

Answer 1

The failure of RBS can be explained by a combination of key factors:

Capital

Significant weaknesses in RBS's capital position came as a result of management decisions and was permitted by an inadequate regulatory capital framework. RBS's capital position was far weaker, in terms of its ability to absorb losses, than its published total regulatory capital resources suggested. This reflected a definition of regulatory capital, which was severely deficient, combined with an RBS strategy of being 'lightly capitalised' relative to its peers.

Liquidity and reliance upon wholesale funding

RBS was over reliant on risky short-term wholesale funding. The whole banking system, but RBS in particular, was excessively dependent on short-term wholesale funding. This dependence was allowed by deficient regulatory and supervisory frameworks, with a seriously flawed liquidity regime to measure, monitor and limit firms' liquidity risks. It also reflected RBS's belief that it would always be able to fund itself, a belief which subsequently proved mistaken.

Asset quality

There were asset quality concerns and uncertainties arising from aggressive growth. Substantial losses in complex credit trading activities eroded market confidence. RBS's strategy underestimated how bad the potential size of losses associated with structured credit might be. Uncertainties about the scale of future loan losses, in addition to those already incurred and potential further credit trading losses, contributed to the loss of confidence in RBS in autumn 2008. The scale of RBS's losses in this area reflected deficient strategy and execution at the firm.

Acquisition of ABN AMRO

The ABN AMRO acquisition significantly increased RBS's exposure to risky asset categories, reduced an already relatively low capital ratio, increased potential liquidity strains and, because of RBS's role as the consortium leader and consolidator, created additional potential and perceived risks. RBS's decision to proceed with this acquisition was made on the basis of due diligence which was inadequate in scope and depth given the nature and scale of the acquisition and the major risks involved. The FSA's overall supervisory response to the acquisition was also inadequate.

Management, governance and culture

The multiple poor decisions that RBS made suggest that there are likely to have been underlying deficiencies in RBS management, governance and culture which made it prone to make poor decisions. Many of the decisions that RBS made appear poor only with the benefit of hindsight but a pattern of decisions that may reasonably be considered poor, at the time or with hindsight, suggests underlying deficiencies in

- The bank's management capabilities and style

- Its governance arrangements

- Checks and balances

- Failings for oversight and challenge and in its culture, particularly its attitude to the balance between risk and growth.

It is difficult, to be certain how aspects of RBS's management, governance and culture affected the quality of its decision-making, but it prompts the following questions. Whether:

- The Board's mode of operation, including challenge to the executive, was as effective as its composition and formal processes suggested.

- The CEO's management style discouraged robust and effective challenge.

- RBS was overly focused on revenue, profit and earnings per share rather than on capital, liquidity and asset quality.

- The Board designed a CEO remuneration package which made it rational to focus on ROE, profitability and growth.

- The Board received adequate information to consider the risks associated with strategy proposals, and whether it was sufficiently disciplined in questioning and challenging what was presented to it.

- Risk management information enabled the Board adequately to monitor and mitigate the aggregation of risks across the group, and whether it was sufficiently forward-looking to give early warning of emerging risks.

Potential areas of concern about RBS's management, governance and culture were identified by the FSA Supervision Team. The degree of supervisory intensity applied to these issues, however, whilst consistent with the FSA's prevailing practices and approach, was less than the regulators now consider appropriate.

Answer 2

The failure of HBOS plc can be explained by a combination of factors. Certain features of HBOS's strategy included:

- A return on equity goal of around 20%
- Aggressive growth targets
- Gaining a market share of 15-20% in all the key markets in which it was involved.

The Group put itself under pressure to maintain an increasing level of income. As margins declined on all forms of lending, a search for yield pushed it towards more risky propositions. Each of the lending divisions experienced an increase in its risk profile as it sought to grow income levels. Key strategic decisions were taken by the Board which aggravated rather than improved the overall risk profile.

Capital

While regulatory capital ratios remained stable and looked robust, leverage had increased for HBOS. At the end of 2007, HBOS had £1 of shareholders' equity supporting every £30 of assets. If account is taken of the significant commitments which were not on the firm's balance sheet, the true leverage of the firm was significantly higher than 30:1. With a smaller proportion of capital supporting an ever growing balance sheet, the potential impact of a downturn on the HBOS increased.

Liquidity and reliance upon wholesale funding

By the end of September 2008, HBOS was no longer able to meet its needs from the wholesale market and was facing a withdrawal of customer deposits and the rapid expansion of its balance sheet placed pressure on HBOS's ability to fund itself. The management and Board of HBOS recognised that an over reliance on wholesale funding was a weakness but this was never tackled as a key risk to the stability of the business. Instead, the possible need for additional funding was viewed as a risk to further asset growth. Higher levels of customer deposits were seen as a way of increasing lending capacity rather than reducing liquidity risk. In addition, the ongoing closure of the syndication market meant that the corporate division was unable to sell-on, as originally intended, significant large exposures that it had agreed to underwrite in full.

Asset quality

Within Corporate, despite the deteriorating economic outlook in 2008, the business functions were reluctant to accept that the loans were going bad, and were reluctant to re-categorise and escalate them to the division's specialist 'impaired assets' team. As more and more corporate loans deteriorated, the division's impaired assets team became overwhelmed with their sheer volume and was unable to properly re-categorise the loans in a timely fashion. The corporate division's proposed levels of provisions did not reflect the declining market conditions, and were increased following intensive discussions with the firm's external auditors. Even then, HBOS consistently chose the level of provisions at the least prudent end of the range deemed acceptable by its external auditors.

Formation of strategy and risk appetite

One of the key factors in the demise of HBOS was the failure to establish an appropriate strategy for the Group, set in the context of clearly identified risks and measures to quantify and control risk. The Board played a limited role in the development of the Group business strategy and delegated responsibility for strategic planning to its CEO using its annual divisional business planning process as the main mechanism for reviewing the Group's strategy. This meant that discussions about the firm's strategy and risk appetite tended to focus on performance targets. The ineffectiveness of HBOS's risk management framework was a consequence of a culture within the firm that prioritised growth aspirations over the consideration of risk. HBOS's weak risk culture was evident with growth setting the tone for the rest of the organisation. The early success of HBOS in the benign economic conditions prior to the crisis also led to complacency during the crisis.

Another key feature of HBOS's failure was that the internal controls within its operating divisions were ineffective and did not keep pace with the rapid growth that these divisions experienced. The impact of these deficiencies was exacerbated by the ineffectiveness of the firm's Group control functions. Challenge from Group internal audit was limited, with some evidence that internal audit reports could be upgraded based on promises from the business to make improvements. The Board delegated responsibility for the firm's overall systems and controls to the Group CEO.

Management, governance and culture

As a group, the non-executive directors (NEDs) on the Board lacked sufficient experience and knowledge of banking. Of the twelve NEDs who served on the Board during the review period only one had a background in banking. This lack of experience hindered the NEDs' ability to provide effective challenge to executive management. As a result, risk was given insufficient time, attention, focus and priority by the Board. The lack of experience and knowledge of banking amongst the NEDs was compounded by a similar lack of banking experience within the executive management team.

Multiple Choice Answers

1 **D** Liquidity measures the extent to which an organisation has sufficient cash to meet its immediate and short-term obligations when they fall due

2 **A** ABCP is a type of commercial paper for which other financial instruments stand as collateral

3 **A** The SRR gave substantial powers to the tripartite regulators to deal with and stabilise banks that are in financial difficulty

4 **B** The ELA scheme is a short term liquidity programme provided by central banks

5 **C** Asset back securities are a financial security that is collateralised by assets such as bonds, loan repayments, leases or property

6 **C** LCR requires banks to have sufficient high quality liquid assets to withstand a stressed funding scenario of 30 days

7   **B**   A mono-line is where a company provides insurance or guarantee against the risk that a bond or other security will default

8   **C**   RMBSs are a type of mortgage backed debt obligation whose cash flows come from a pool of mortgage related loans

9   **B**   The Sterling Stock Regime required banks to have sufficient high quality liquid stocks to withstand a stressed funding scenario of two days

10   **B**   The most important feature which distinguished failed banks from survivor banks during the banking crisis was leverage

Chapter 3 – Post Crisis Regulation

Answer 1

The main powers that have been granted to the FCA include:

- Approving persons in the industry to perform in certain controlled functions for example approving the senior board management of banks

- Imposing penalties for market abuse

- Taking disciplinary action

- Authorising unit trust schemes and recognising collective investment schemes

- Recognising investment exchanges

- Keeping under review the desirability of regulating the Lloyds insurance market and designated professional bodies

- Making rules

- Demanding information from authorised persons

- Conducting investigations with HM Treasury

- Instituting criminal proceedings where necessary

- Maintaining a public record of authorised persons, schemes, prohibited individuals and approved persons

- Initiating or participating in insolvency proceedings

- Cooperating with other regulators.

Answer 2

The Turner Review took an in-depth look at the causes of the financial crisis, and recommended steps that the international community needed to take to enhance regulatory standards, supervisory approaches and international cooperation and coordination.

The Review focused on long-term solutions rather than the short-term challenges and distinguished areas where the regulator had already taken action; those where the UK could proceed nationally; and those where we needed to achieve international agreement.

The Review identified three underlying causes of the crisis:

1 Macroeconomic imbalances
2 Financial innovation of little social value
3 Significant deficiencies in bank capital and liquidity regulations.

The Review emphasised the importance of regulation and supervision being based on a 'macro-prudential' (system-wide) approach rather than focussing solely on specific firms.

The Turner Review made the following recommendations:

- Fundamental changes to bank capital and liquidity regulations and to banks' published accounts

- More and higher quality bank capital, with several times as much capital required to support risky trading activity

- Counter-cyclical capital buffers, building up in good economic times so that they can be drawn on in downturns, and reflected in published account estimates of future potential losses

- A central role for much tighter regulation of liquidity

- Regulation of 'shadow banking' activities on the basis of economic substance not legal form: increased reporting requirements for unregulated financial institutions such as hedge funds, and regulator powers to extend capital regulation

- Regulation of credit rating agencies to limit conflicts of interest and inappropriate application of rating techniques

- National and international action to ensure that remuneration policies are designed to discourage excessive risk taking

- Major changes in the regulators supervisory approach, building on the existing Supervisory Enhancement Programme (SEP), with a focus on business strategies and system-wide risks, rather than internal processes and structures

- Major reforms in the regulation of the European banking market, combining a new European regulatory authority and increased national powers to constrain risky cross-border activity

The transition to higher bank capital would need to be managed carefully. Lord Turner noted that UK banks were already capitalised at a level which would enable them to absorb 'severe stresses': the short-term priority would be to maintain bank lending to the real economy.

Answer 3

According to the Treasury Select Committee, the origins of the banking crisis were many and varied, including:

- Low real interest rates
- A search for yield
- Apparent excess liquidity
- And a misplaced faith in financial innovation.

These ingredients combined to create an environment rich in over-confidence, over-optimism and the stifling of contrary opinions. Notwithstanding this febrile environment, some of the banks, not just RBS and HBOS, have been the principal authors of their own demise.

The culture within large parts of British banking has increasingly been one of risk taking leading to the meltdown that we have witnessed. Bankers have made an astonishing mess of the financial system. However, this was a failure not only within individual banks but also of the supervisory system designed to protect the public from systemic risk.

Multiple Choice Answers

1	D	The Financial Services (Banking Reform) Bill focussed on changing the structure and delivery of regulation within the financial services
2	C	The Bank of England is committed to promote and maintain monetary and financial stability
3	A	The Bank of England reports to Parliament through the Treasury Select Committee
4	C	The Financial Policy Committee is charged with identifying, monitoring and removing systemic risk within the banking system
5	B	The FPC is able is able to make recommendations and give direction to both the FCA and PRA
6	B	The PRA is responsible for the regulation and supervision of banks

7	**B**	The FCA is responsible for ensuring markets work well so that consumers get a good deal
8	**D**	The Vickers Report considered the structural and non-structural reforms needed to promote financial stability and competition in the UK banking sector
9	**C**	The NSF ratio is a long term structural ratio designed to address liquidity mismatches
10	**C**	'Wrong way' risk arises when default risk and credit exposure increase together

Chapter 4 – Corporate Social Responsibility and Sustainability

Answer 1

The five sustainability considerations relevant to operations management are:

1   The first consideration concerns the level of world population that should be sustained and the needs of developing countries. An operations management consideration is, for example, whether organisations should source products from developing nations or look to the tried and tested industries of developed countries.

2   The second consideration is about things such as the environment, employees and/or economic factors.

    (a)   Ecological sustainability concerns the preservation of the environment so it can function as naturally as possible. The operations management issue is whether organisations should continue production processes which are harmful to the environment, or should they look for other less harmful (but possibly more expensive) alternatives.

    (b)   Social sustainability is about personal growth and development. For organisations the issue is whether employees should be treated like machines by requiring them to perform repetitive tasks, or should they be given scope to develop their abilities and perform a wide range of production roles.

    (c)   Economic sustainability is about producing goods and services that people want while maximising the organisation's profitability. The operations issue here is to ensure the organisation produces products and services that its customers want while minimising waste to maximise profit.

3   The third consideration concerns the issue of generational equity. This is about ensuring future generations can enjoy the same environmental conditions as the current generation, and that social welfare is maintained or increased. The main operations management concern is the use of natural materials. As the world has finite resources, production levels cannot be sustained forever. Therefore organisations need to plan their use of resources carefully, especially the rate at which they use them. They should also look for new ways of producing the products that people want, as well as looking for sustainable resources.

4   The fourth consideration is about the balance that has to be found between preserving the environment and natural resources with the need to produce goods and services. The operations management issue concerns sourcing materials which balance the need for sustainability with the need to produce goods and services. For example, organisations can look at substituting some raw materials with sustainable alternatives or look to produce products using more sustainable processes.

5   The last consideration is about responsibility. Ideally, the whole world will take responsibility for sustainability, but this is unlikely due to a lack of meaningful global international agreements. The operations management issue is that organisations must take on responsibility for sustainability themselves rather than waiting for legal regulation.

Answer 2

The Chartered Banker Professional Standards Board (CB:PSB) is a voluntary joint initiative by eight leading banks in the UK and the Chartered Banker Institute. It was established in 2011 and was set up to:

- Develop a series of professional standards to support the ethical awareness, customer focus and competence of those working in the banking industry

- Facilitate industry and public awareness and recognition of the standards

- Establish mechanisms for the implementation, monitoring and enforcement of the standards

- Help build, over time, greater public confidence and trust in individuals, institutions and the banking industry overall, and enhance pride in the banking profession.

In summary, the Boards overall aim is to restore public confidence and trust in the industry, and promote a culture of professionalism amongst individual bankers by creating industry wide standards for professional knowledge, skills and competence.

Answer 3

CSR and sustainability initiatives will affect many aspects of a business's operations including:

1 **Design and delivery of products and services**

   Operations should consider the impact of products and services at the design stage, for example, the benefits and costs on society and the environmental impact at all stages of a product or service's life. This means the resources used and waste created in the design and delivery of stage, plus the use and eventual disposal of the product by the customer should be considered. The provision of recycling facilities and information on materials used in a product are ways that a business can show social responsibility.

2 **Capacity management**

   Waste and energy use by the organisation can be minimised if demand is managed and the organisation operates at an efficient level of capacity. This will mean that output meets actual demand and products or services will not be produced unnecessarily.

3 **Inventory management**

   Inventory levels should be as efficient as possible. Storing materials for long periods of time is costly in terms of resources (such as energy) and potential wastage (if products have a limited life). Therefore operations should seek to hold the minimum levels of inventory.

4 **Quality management**

   Poor quality results in wasted resources in terms of materials used in production and energy used in the production process. Therefore, operations should seek to minimise poor quality. If wastage does occur then materials should be recycled as much as possible and if necessary disposed in an environmentally friendly way.

5 **Supply chain management**

   The design and management of supply chains can have a significant impact on the resources used in the production process and on society. Businesses should recognise that they have a responsibility to take appropriate steps to help reduce the environmental impact of their suppliers as well as themselves. Large organisations can show some social responsibility by using local suppliers where possible. This will help support the local economy and reduce the amount of resources used in transporting materials.

Multiple Choice Answers

1	**A**	The ability of financial markets to keep going is based on confidence
2	**D**	CSR is a form of corporate self-regulation integrated into a business model
3	**C**	CSR can be described as an obligation, beyond that required by the law, for a business to pursue long-term goals that are good for society
4	**B**	The BSB was established to promote high standards of ethical behaviour and competence across the banking sector
5	**B**	Delivering the right outcome for customers is critical and that means replacing the 'product push' approach of the past with a product life cycle approach
6	**A**	A socially responsible organisation should be an ethical organisation
7	**C**	CSR is about responsibility to all stakeholders
8	**C**	FSC provides a State guarantee to customers of failed institutions
9	**D**	Ethics is concerned with morally correct behaviour
10	**D**	Large organisations can show some social responsibility by using local suppliers where possible

Chapter 5 – Banking Operational Models and Service Quality

Answer 1

Mission statements are likely to have some of the following characteristics:

- Stating the purpose of the organisation
- Stating the business areas in which the organisation intends to operate
- Providing a general statement of the organisation's culture
- Acting as a guide to develop the direction of the strategy and its goals/objectives

Lynch (Strategic Management, 2015) provided the following criteria by which to judge the effectiveness of a corporate mission statement:

- Is it specific enough to impact upon individuals' behaviour throughout the business?

- Does it reflect the distinctive advantage of the organisation and recognise its strengths and weaknesses?

- Is it realistic and attainable?

- Is it flexible to the demands of a changing environment?

Answer 2

Mission statements can play an important role in the strategic planning process.

- To inspire and inform planning. Plans should further the organisation's goals and be consistent with its values. In this way, the mission statement provides a focus for consistent strategic planning decisions.

- To act as a yardstick by which plans are judged.

- Mission statements also affect the implementation of a planned strategy in terms of the ways in which an organisation carries out its business, and through the culture of the organisation. A mission statement can help to develop a corporate culture in an organisation by communicating the organisation's core values.

- To help to establish an ethics framework.

An understanding of an organisation's mission is invaluable for setting and controlling the overall functioning and progress of the organisation. By designing efficient and effective processes, and making good use of value chains and supply chains, the maximum output can be generated for the least input.

Answer 3

The five key gaps are:

Gap 1: Exists because there is a difference between the levels of service that the customer expects to receive and management's interpretation of the customer's expectations. Market research, feedback from frontline staff and customer complaints are useful indicators here. An example might be the size and scope of activity of a bank. Bank executives may see size as a service strength, while a customer might see this as a disadvantage because bigger could imply a more impersonal level of service.

Gap 2: This may result from management being unsuccessful in translating the customer's requirements of service quality into service quality standards for the bank for staff to follow. For example, managers might think customers want to see a bank manager when they have a complaint; whilst customers may prefer the complaint to be dealt with remotely, quickly and with the minimum of fuss.

Gap 3: This exists because the actual service delivery, before or after the event, has failed to meet the defined standards. It is not possible to ensure exactly the same quality of delivery for services as opposed to manufactured products; largely because of the people element.

Gap 4: Can arise if the levels of service are not properly communicated or understood by the customer. Often, when pitching for business some will put their most senior staff in front of the potential clients. If the business is won, these more senior staff may then disappear into the background, so setting the right levels of involvement, expectations and communicating this at the outset is a key requirement.

Gap 5: Exists if the customer's perception of the service that is being provided falls short of what they hoped for. An example here might be the bank failing to provide adequate information on a particular service to which the customer had discussed at a previous meeting.

In reality, some gaps are inevitable; the challenge is not to make them transparent to customers.

Multiple Choice Answers

1	**B**	The Ashridge Mission model of mission statements links business strategy to culture and ethics
2	**A**	Horizontal integration is using current capabilities by developing into activities that are competitive with, or directly complementary, to its present activities
3	**B**	Vertical integration is when a company expands backwards or forwards within its existing value network and therefore becomes its own supplier or distributor
4	**A**	Analytics are designed to produce intelligence, not information
5	**D**	Service quality is defined as meeting or exceeding customers' expectations at a price that is acceptable to the customer and at a return that is acceptable to the organisation
6	**B**	Service quality gaps can emerge because of misunderstanding, misinterpretation or mismanagement
7	**B**	The essence of good customer service is that the buyer and supplier develop a mutually beneficial relationship
8	**A**	An SLA is a part of a service contract where the level of service is clearly defined
9	**C**	Studies show that 80% of customers who defected to competitors had scored themselves as being 'satisfied' or 'very satisfied' in customer satisfaction surveys
10	**A**	Customer loyalty is the intention to stay

Chapter 6 – Operational Risk Management

Answer 1

Increasingly, banks are adopting 'three lines of defence' in embedding risk management capability across their organisation. The model distinguishes between functions that own and manage risks, functions overseeing risks and functions providing independent assurance.

The first line of defence is the business operations itself; risk and control in the business lines. It describes the controls that an organisation has in place to deal with the day-to-day business; in effect the line management. Risk controls are designed into systems and processes. Assuming that the design is sound to mitigate risk appropriately, compliance with process should ensure an adequate control environment. This first line of defence provides management assurance, and informs the audit committee by identifying risks and business improvement actions, implementing controls, and reporting on progress.

The second line of defence is the combination of the risk management and compliance functions. Here the risk management functions facilitate and monitor the implementation of effective risk management practices by operational management. This also assists the risk owners (line managers) in reporting adequate risk-related information and provides oversight over business process and risks. The second line is re-enforced by the advisory and monitoring functions of risk management and compliance.

The third line of defence is audit (internal audit and other independent external assurance providers). This describes the independent assurance provided by the board audit committee, a committee of non-executive directors chaired by the senior independent director, and the internal audit function that reports to that committee. Internal audit undertakes a programme of risk-based audits covering all aspects of both first and second lines of defence. Internal audit may well take some assurance from the work of the second line functions and reduce or tailor its checking of the first line.

Answer 2

There are a number of operational risk event types are those which the Basel Committee in co-operation with the banking industry which have been identified as having the potential to result in substantial losses. These are then used within Basel as the basis for the operational loss database, which follows the business lines and analyses losses accordingly. These are the main areas where substantial losses are anticipated.

There are eight business lines defined by the Basel Committee which are applicable to banks. They are:

1   Corporate finance
2   Trading and sales
3   Retail banking
4   Commercial banking
5   Payments and settlement
6   Agency services
7   Asset management
8   Retail brokerage.

From time to time the Basel Committee carries out reviews of operational risk loss data collection across a large number of banks. These studies deliver hard data showing the frequency by risk type and also across different business lines. The highest numbers of risk events have been proved to occur amongst external fraud and the execution and delivery and processes.

Answer 3

The benefits of sound operational risk management within banks can be summarised as follows:

- A reduction of operating losses
- Lower compliance/auditing costs
- The early detection of unlawful activities
- Reduced exposure to future risks
- A lower capital charge under the regulatory environment in line with Basel recommendations
- Better decision making
- Improved credit ratings, share price and reputation.

These benefits lead to greater resilience in the business and a better chance of the business growing and attracting further customers in line with its strategic objectives.

Answer 4

There are various benefits that also spin off from the actual activity of operational risk. These are:

- Improved operational risk governance
- Improvements to risk and control assessment
- Better data capture, record keeping and analysis
- Improvements in stress testing and scenario planning leading to better modelling
- Better reporting and priority setting
- Greater clarity over risk appetite and tolerance
- Ability to use risk indicators more effectively.

A bank that utilises sound operational risk management will benefit in further ways beyond merely the risk management framework. It will also be able to attract and retain better quality staff to improve its resilience and business continuity.

Answer 5

The risk policy of any organisation should aim to:

- Employ a methodology that identifies and categorises all the operational risks that exist in the organisation.

- Employ a methodology for measuring and assessing the significance of all the identified risks.

- Work with line managers to agree the mitigating action required to reduce the risk exposure to acceptable levels.

- Monitor the effects of the mitigating action to ensure its success.

- Report and escalate risk issues to all levels of the organisation. This ensures that there is transparency and aids the decision-making process.

Multiple Choice Answers

1	B	Banks must report to the FCA on complaints received every six months
2	B	The Basel Committee defines operational risk as the risk of loss resulting from inadequate or failed internal processes, people and systems or from external events
3	A	The responsibility of the risk control framework and corporate governance lies with the Board
4	B	The Chief Risk Officer is accountable to both the Executive Committee and the Board

5	**C**	The purpose of an audit is to provide an independent review
6	**D**	An external audit will report to the members and shareholders of a company
7	**B**	The PRA rules state that 'a firm should ensure that all employees are aware of their responsibility and role in operational risk management and are suitable and capable of performing these responsibilities'

Chapter 7 – Operational Management

Answer 1

According to Quinn and Hilmer the three tests to establish whether an activity should be outsourced are:

1   Potential for competitive advantage. The lower the potential for competitive advantage, the more suitable an activity is for outsourcing.

2   Strategic risk (or vulnerability) and the need for flexibility. Where strategic risk is high, or where an organisation is vulnerable, the activity should be kept in-house. However, where strategic risk is low and the need for flexibility is high, then the activity should be outsourced on a short-term contract.

3   Transaction costs. The level of transaction costs should be input into the decision.

Answer 2

The stages are:

1   **Reacting**: departments optimise their operations to meet demand. Reacting organisations cannot sense demand or tie it into corporate strategy; they simply react to market conditions.

2   **Anticipating**: anticipating companies have developed internally to respond to long and short-term demand. They often use lean production or six sigma to bring order to their operations. They can anticipate upstream demand (the demand which is coming to them) but not downstream demand.

3   **Collaborating**: collaborating organisations have established external relationships with business partners that allow intelligence to be gathered on downstream demand. This allows better forecasting and adjustment of plans.

4   **Orchestrating**: supply and demand have evolved into a flow of information throughout the network. Companies plan new products and product life cycles, and can begin to influence demand patterns. Production decisions are based on costs and profitability.

Answer 3

The aim is to co-ordinate the whole chain, from raw material suppliers to end customers. The chain should be considered as a network rather than a pipeline, a network of vendors support a network of customers, with third parties such as transport businesses helping to link the companies. In marketing channels, organisations have to manage the trade-off between the desire to remain independent and autonomous, and the need to be interdependent and co-operative.

- **Independence**: each channel member operates in isolation and is not affected by others, so maintains a greater degree of control.

- **Interdependence**: each channel member can affect the performance of others in the channel.

If the supplier 'knows' what its customers want, it does not necessarily have to guess, or wait until the customer places an order. It will be able to better plan its own delivery systems.

The potential for using the Internet to allow customers and suppliers to acquire up-to-date information about forecasted needs and delivery schedules is a recent development, but one which is being used by an increasing number of companies. Some supply chain relationships are strengthened and communication facilitated through the use of extranets (intranets accessible to authorised outsiders).

Multiple Choice Answers

1 **D** The main objective of operational risk is to use a transformation process to add value and create competitive advantage

2 **D** The value a business adds does not arises from activities and processes

3 **C** According to Porter, business activities are not the same as business functions

4 **C** According to Porter, primary activities are those directly related to production, sales, marketing, delivery and services

5 **D** Process mapping aims to identify and represent the steps and decisions involved in a process

6 **D** Operational management tries to ensure that organisations are run efficiently

7 **C** Translating business or market strategy into an operations strategy requires competitive factors

8 **C** Strategies should be continually reviewed in response to changes in the environment

9 **D** Kotler believed that meeting customer requirements as identifying value, delivering value and communicating value

10 **A** Porter's value chain is a model of value activities

Chapter 8 – Quality Management

Answer 1

Prevention: organisations should take measures that prevent poor quality occurring.

Right first time: a culture should be developed that encourages workers to get their work right first time, every time.

Eliminate waste: the organisation should seek the most efficient and effective use of all its resources

Continuous improvement: the Kaizen philosophy should be adopted. Organisations should seek to improve their processes continually.

Everyone's concern: everyone in the organisation is responsible for improving processes and systems under their control, including a commitment to quality from senior management.

Participation: all workers should be encouraged to share their views and the organisation should listen to and value them.

Teamwork and empowerment: workers across departments should form team bonds so that eventually the organisation becomes one.

Answer 2

Lean production or lean process improvement involves the systematic elimination of waste, such as:

- **Over production and early production**
- **Waiting**: time delays, idle time, any time during which value is not added to the product
- **Transportation**: multiple handling, delay in materials handling, unnecessary handling
- **Inventory**: holding or purchasing unnecessary raw materials, work in process and finished goods
- **Motion**: actions of people or equipment that do not add value to the product
- **Over processing**: unnecessary steps or work elements/procedures (non-added value work)
- **Defective units**: production of a part that is scrapped or requires rework

Lean production focuses on reducing system response time so that the production system is capable of rapid change to meet market demands.

Answer 3

Supporters of lean production believe it enables a company to deliver on demand, minimise inventory, maximise the use of multi-skilled employees, flatten the management structure and focus resources where they are most effective.

Other benefits include:

- Waste reduction
- Production cost reduction
- Manufacturing cycle times decreased
- Labour reduction while maintaining or increasing throughput
- Inventory reduction while increasing customer service levels
- Capacity increase in current facilities
- Higher quality
- Higher profits
- Higher system flexibility in reacting to changes in requirements improved
- More strategic focus
- Improved cash flow through increasing shipping and billing frequencies

Answer 4

SERVQUAL was developed in the 1980s by Zeithaml, Parasuraman and Berry as a method of measuring quality in service organisations.

It was primarily concerned with measuring the gap between a customer's preconceived expectations and the actual experience they receive. It measures ten aspects of service quality:

1   Understanding the customer
2   Tangibles
3   Courtesy
4   Security
5   Credibility
6   Competence
7   Communication
8   Access
9   Reliability
10   Responsiveness

Multiple Choice Answers

1	**C**	Quality is concerned with fitness for purpose
2	**C**	Quality management is responsible for ensuring that products or services meet their planned level of quality and conform to specifications
3	**D**	Modern approaches to quality focus on the prevention of defects through quality standards and processes
4	**B**	The balanced scorecard focuses on four different perspectives: customer; internal operations; innovation and learning; and financial
5	**B**	Continuous improvement is sometimes referred to as Kaizen
6	**C**	Six Sigma is designed to help organisations focus on developing and delivering near-perfect products and services
7	**A**	Lean production involves identifying and eliminating all non value-adding activities
8	**A**	Discipline, simplicity, pride, standardisation and repeatability are emphasised as being critical to efficiency in the 5S model
9	**C**	A key feature of world class manufacturing is flexibility of production
10	**D**	Quality control is concerned with checking and reviewing work that has been done

Chapter 9 – Quality Management Techniques

Answer 1

Visual management helps to:

- Understand and indicate work priorities
- See whether performance is being met
- Identify the flow of work and what is being done
- Identify when something is going wrong or is not happening
- Show what the standards of work should be
- Communicates to everyone what performance measures are in place
- Provide real time feedback to everyone involved.

Answer 2

A SOP is an agreed written procedure which lists all the steps of an operation, in their correct order. It tells us exactly what that process involves by explaining not only **what** to do, but **how** to do it. It provides confidence and assurance that the same level of high service will be provided to every customer by every team. The SOP identifies critical points, quality checks and any process aids or tools needed to complete the operation correctly. It captures all process knowledge and expertise creating a standardised process for all to follow. It also ensures that important controls are being adhered to prevent risk failure for the bank.

Answer 3

SOPs benefit the customer and the workplace by:

- Reducing variations within processes leading to a reduction in errors and an improved customer experience

- Reducing processing times as standard times are more likely to be achieved by everyone

- Improving the ability to plan ahead as performance becomes more predictable

- Helping to train new staff to learn and understand the teams processes more effectively

- Improving processes, through the sharing of best practices and customer/team feedback thereby reducing complaints and performance/quality failures

- Ensuring the benefits of any improvement activities are sustained.

- Making things simple for everyone

- Saving time, effort and cost

- Creating a culture of 'find the waste and eliminate it'; it provides a benchmark for improvement.

The SOP document is made available to everyone so that they can adopt and consistently replicate the one best way of doing the job and the right people to define the one best way are the users. Real business benefits can accrue if you can capture and standardise the one best way.

Answer 4

Problems can be defined as:

- A deviation from standard
- A doubtful or difficult task
- Something that is hard to understand
- A Service Level Agreement not being met
- Increased customer complaints
- Decrease in quality of work.

And can arise from:

- Customer complaints
- Internal audit
- Coaching sessions
- Team observations
- Quality control metrics.

Multiple Choice Answers

1 **A** Lean defines a problem as a gap to a standard

2 **D** P&Cs ensure that problems and issues are identified, understood and managed consistently

3 **C** A tally sheet is used to gather data to help in assessing the situation and to focus on the real issues

4 **C** Swim-lane process maps are the best tool for identifying the work flows across several teams, departments or people

5 **A** Brainstorming allows the team to generate ideas and boost creativity

6 **D** The priority matrix is based on ease of implementation and the size of the impact

7 **C** Validating is the check part of the PDCA cycle

8 **C** In SOP, standardisation means finding the one best way of doing things and getting everyone to do it that way

9 **C** A SWOT analysis seeks to turn threats into opportunities

10 **D** The PDCA cycle can be used as a model to measure improvement activity

Chapter 10 – Management Accounting and Management Information

Answer 1

Budgets can be useful for a number of reasons:

- **Co-ordination**: ensures managers work together in the best interests of the organisation.

- **Responsibility**: sets out which managers are responsible for controlling which costs and authorises them to do so.

- **Utilisation**: helps managers make efficient and effective use of the resources under their control.

- **Motivation**: helps to motivate managers to act in the best interests of the organisation by aligning their goals with those of the organisation.

- **Planning**: managers are forced to look to the future, to identify opportunities and threats and consider ways of tackling them.

- **Evaluation**: forms a basis for performance appraisal of managers.

- **Communication**: the plans are communicated to individuals within the business so that all know what they are expected to do.

It should be noted that several of these uses (in particular, motivation and planning) are only relevant if managers are involved in the budgeting process, rather than where managers have budgets imposed on them.

Answer 2

ACCURATE stands for:

Accurate: figures in a report should add up, the degree of rounding should be appropriate, there should be no typos, items should be allocated to the correct category, assumptions should be stated for uncertain information. It must be reliable.

Complete: information should include everything relevant to the decision being considered. If relevant, comparative information should be included. Information should be consistent, for example it should be collected on the same basis each time, to allow for meaningful comparison. Excessive information should be avoided.

Cost-effective: it should not cost more to obtain the information than the benefit derived from its use. Information collection and analysis should be efficient. Presentation should be clear, such that users do not waste time working out what the information means.

Understandable: the needs of the user are paramount. The information must be easy to read and well presented.

Relevant: information that is not needed for a decision should be omitted. All significant information that is relevant to the decision being considered must be included.

Accessible: the choice of medium to provide the information should be appropriate (face-to-face, email, letter, written report) and consider the needs of the user.

Timely: the information should be available when it is needed and in time for required action to be effective.

Easy to use: as well as being understandable (clear and well presented) and accessible (correct choice of medium) the information should be presented in a manner that the user can easily use or pass on as required.

Information systems should aim to produce information that possesses all these qualities.

Answer 3

The Lending Code is a self-regulatory lending code setting minimum standards of good practice when dealing with the following customers in the UK:

- Consumers
- Micro-enterprises
- Charities with an annual income of less than £1 million.

As a self-regulatory code, it allows competition and market forces to work to encourage higher standards for the benefit of customers.

The Lending Code covers good practice in relation to:

- Loans
- Credit cards
- Charge cards
- Current account overdrafts.

The Code sets standards of good lending practice.

Multiple Choice Answers

1   **B**   Financial accounting is concerned with stewardship

2   **B**   Management accounting differs from financial accounting because it emphasises purpose rather than techniques

3   **C**   A budget is a plan of revenues and expenses that the organisation expects for a forthcoming period

4   **B**   Environmental scanning is the process of gathering external information from a wide range of sources

5   **B**   Transaction processing systems are used for routine tasks in which data items or transactions must be processed so that operations can continue

6   **D**   Executive information systems are used by pooling data from internal and external sources and makes information available to senior managers in an easy-to-use form

7   **A**   Decision support systems are used by management to assist in making decisions on issues which are subject to high levels of uncertainty

8   **C**   Knowledge work systems are used to facilitate the creation and integration of new knowledge into an organisation

9   **C**   Office automation systems (OAS) are computer systems designed to increase the productivity of data and information workers

10   **B**   Compliance with the Lending Code is enforced by the Lending Standards Board

Chapter 11 – Capacity Management

Answer 1

Cost: costs are affected by planned capacity. When the capacity of an operation exceeds demand, there will be under-utilised resources and costs will be higher than if capacity were more closely matched to demand.

Revenue: if demand exceeds the capacity of an operation to meet it, revenues will be forgone that could otherwise have been earned.

Quality: the quality of an operation could be affected by capacity planning. For example, if an operation varies its capacity by using part-time or temporary staff, the quality of the product or service might be compromised.

Speed of response to demand: the speed of response can be improved either by building up finished goods inventories or by providing sufficient capacity to avoid customers having to queue or to wait.

Dependability of supply: the closer an operation works to its capacity limit, the less easily it will be able to cope with unexpected disruptions to the work flow. Supply will therefore be less dependable.

Flexibility: the flexibility of an operation, and in particular its ability to vary the volume of output it can produce, will be improved by having surplus capacity. An operation working at or close to its capacity limit is much less flexible.

Answer 2

MRP I is a technique for deciding the volume and timing of materials in manufacturing conditions where there is dependent demand.

The purpose of an MRP I system is to:

- Calculate the quantity of materials required, for each type of material
- Determine when they will be required.

The materials requirements are calculated from:

- Known future orders, i.e. firm orders already received from customers
- A forecast of other future orders that, with a reasonable degree of confidence, will be received.

The quantities of each type of materials required for the product or service will be defined in its bill of materials. Estimates of firm and likely demand can therefore be converted into a materials requirements schedule.

MRP I enables manufacturing organisations to determine when to order material by working back from when they will be required for production, and allowing the necessary lead time for production or for purchasing from an external supplier.

There are numerous benefits to an organisation which uses an MRP I system. For example, it can reduce its inventory levels while being able to meet orders, the system can identify and warn of production problems such as bottlenecks, and it can assist with Just in time (JIT) management by forging close relationships with suppliers.

Answer 3

MRP II is a plan for anticipating and monitoring all the resources of a manufacturing company such as manufacturing, marketing, finance and engineering. It is a computerised system that incorporates a single database used by many different areas of the organisation each functions working from a common set of data.

It is a sophisticated system that enables optimal inventory control based on the matching of supply and demand.

Features include:

- Production planning
- Capacity planning
- Forecasting
- Purchasing
- Order-entry
- Operations control
- Financial analysis.

MRP II benefits include:

- Reduced stock-outs, therefore better customer service
- Reduced inventory holding costs
- Improved plant/facilities utilisation
- Reliable order fulfilment times
- Reduced 'crisis management' or fire-fighting time.

Multiple Choice Answers

1	**A**	Capacity management aims to maximise the returns an organisation achieves on the assets and systems it uses
2	**B**	Overcapacity means resources available for production are nor fully utilised
3	**A**	Dependent demand relates to demand that is predictable because it is based on factors that are known
4	**C**	The objective of capacity planning is to maximise both profits and customer satisfaction
5	**B**	Kanban is a form of pull control
6	**A**	With pull control, there should be less inventory in the system
7	**D**	A level capacity plan is aimed at maintaining activity at a constant level over a period ignoring fluctuations in forecast demand
8	**B**	Case demand aims to match capacity to forecast fluctuations in demand
9	**D**	Capacity management is measured in terms of input resources and outputs produced
10	**C**	Sequencing refers to the order that different jobs will be done or orders fulfilled

Chapter 12 – Banking Innovation

Answer 1

Cheque imaging is an innovation that cuts down cheque clearing times by sending a digital image of the cheque for clearing, rather than the paper cheque itself. It will provide greater opportunities for banks and building societies to innovate and provide new services. For example, customers may be able to take a photograph of their cheque on their smartphone and pay it in electronically via their bank's mobile banking app. Customers without smartphones will be able to deposit their cheques as usual at bank branches or cash machines, where a cheque can be scanned and the image transmitted electronically.

The key benefit that cheque imaging will enable is a faster cheque clearing cycle, reduced from six days to as few as two, meaning consumers and businesses will receive their funds more quickly. This will bring cheque clearing times into line with other modern payment systems, and in some instances will be faster than other electronic models, such as Bacs and the card schemes, which can take several days.

The introduction of image capture for cheques will lead to sizeable cost savings for banks and building societies as it will bring the cost of cheque clearing more in line with that of electronic inter-bank and card payment systems.

It therefore represents an opportunity to secure the future of the cheque by making it a cost-effective, sustainable payment option that financial institutions can afford to provide. Furthermore, by reducing or removing the need for courier transportation of cheques between branches, processors and exchanges, cheque imaging will significantly reduce carbon emissions in the financial services sector.

Cheque imaging will also reduce barriers to entry and encourage greater competition in the retail banking market, by putting challenger banks in a better position to compete even if they lack an established physical branch network. The option of paying in cheques via smartphones will make it easier for challengers to compete with the large, incumbent financial institutions, and will offer those institutions with a limited physical presence the opportunity to expand their customer base beyond their traditional brick and mortar footprint.

Answer 2

Advantages of a centralised system or department include:

- Assuming centralised processing is used, there is only one set of files. Everyone uses the same data and information.

- It gives better security/control over data and files and it is easier to enforce standards.

- Head office is in a better position to know what is going on.

- There may be economies of scale available in purchasing computer equipment and supplies.

- Computer staff are in a single location, and more expert staff are likely to be employed. Career paths may be more clearly defined.

Disadvantages of a centralised system or department include:

- Local offices might have to wait for IS/IT services and assistance.
- Reliance on head office. Local offices are less self-sufficient.
- A system fault at head office will impact across the organisation.

Answer 3

Advantages of a decentralised system or department include:

- Each office can introduce an information system specially tailored for its individual needs. Local changes in business requirements can be taken into account.

- Each office is more self-sufficient.

- Offices are likely to have quicker access to IS/IT support/advice.

- A decentralised structure is more likely to facilitate accurate cost/overhead allocations.

The disadvantages of a decentralised system or department include:

- Control may be difficult, as uncoordinated information systems may be introduced.

- Self-sufficiency may encourage a lack of co-ordination between departments.

- Increased risk of data duplication, with different offices holding the same data on their own separate files.

Answer 4

Volume: the volume of data generated is a key feature of Big Data. The quantity of data now being produced is being driven by social media and transactional-based data sets recorded by large organisations, for example data captured from in-store loyalty cards, till receipts and credit card purchases.

Velocity: velocity refers to the speed at which real time data is being streamed into the organisation. To make data meaningful it needs to be processed in a reasonable time frame.

Variety: modern data takes many different forms. Structured data may take the form of numerical data whereas un-structured data may be in the format of email or video. This presents a challenge for organisations as processing varied forms of data requires significant investment in people and IT infrastructure.

Multiple Choice Answers

1	**B**	Customers start to earn interest two days after depositing a cheque
2	**C**	According to the BBA, 80% of UK businesses have an over reliance on bank sourced credit
3	**A**	Cash is the most expensive payment option for retailers
4	**A**	Big Data is used in value creation
5	**D**	The first internet only bank was established in 1995
6	**D**	The payment services regulator seeks to promote competition and innovation in payment services
7	**C**	The aim of shared service centres is to improve back office efficiency
8	**C**	Risk and compliance functions are not usually decentralised
9	**A**	On average, mobile banking customers interact with their bank three times more than online banking customers
10	**A**	Big Data analytics are used to analyse data in order to improve profitability

Chapter 13 – Digitalisation of the Banking Industry

Answer 1

The barriers to the benefit of data analytics include:

Data ownership: it might be difficult to identify the legal owner of the data collected as this could depend on where the data comes from, how it is archived, and whether it is linked to intellectual property rights or data protection requirements. It should be noted that big data has no value in itself, it is the algorithm and analytic ability of the bank which produces the end value. Consequently, it depends on the cost and time invested in the collection, organisation and accessibility of the data, as well as the necessary IT infrastructure and cloud-based technologies needed to store, process and analyse it.

Cloud computing challenges: the financial industry is still in the early stages of cloud adoption due to specific important concerns over security. For the banking sector, public breach notification, security incident, data security, malware and hacking are considered critical risks to be avoided. EU players face certain geolocalisaton and data privacy restrictions whereas US players do not and are able to use data stored on the cloud all over the world. This creates extra burdens and costs to European companies in comparison to players outside Europe that don't have to comply with the same rules (EU Data Protection Regulation) and hence an unlevel playing field.

Employees with the right skills and competencies: 'handling' and 'processing' data rely on innovative solutions involving technological, analytical and interpretation of the data. This requires highly qualified employees such as data strategists, engineers, statisticians, data analysts etc. who need to develop specific analytical skills to deal with complex big data management systems.

Lack of harmonisation among supervisors: it is difficult for banks to benefit fully from the data analytics opportunities as they are subject to specific supervision, whereas businesses not falling under the supervision of financial regulators possess their client's financial data.

Legacy of banks' IT systems' infrastructure: the growing volume, variety and velocity of data needs to be connected throughout organisations and departments in order to give ready access to products and customer information. Some banks may still be working on partly decentralised or fragmented systems. It is important to ensure that banks take full advantage of their infrastructure to share and benefit from internal data across their organisation.

Answer 2

The use of data analytics has many advantages from a customer experience point of view. The data collected, based on customer's informed consent, when required, will improve the understanding of customer's needs, the quality of products and services and facilitate the development of personalised offers in real time. Data analytics also offer opportunities to identify potential warning signs in terms of fraud or creditworthiness assessment.

Given the changes in society and the use of social media, the new generations of customers arrive with fresh expectations. They expect banks to take into account the data, already at their disposal, when offering services. Customers are increasingly willing to accept the sharing of data and are inclined to forego privacy either in exchange for more tailor-made products and services, or, for instant access to them.

Consumers expect banks to be able to deal with financial data in a highly confidential and trustworthy manner. Data analytics, generally, contribute positively to maintaining trust, transparency and security. Banks have a longstanding expertise in dealing with trust, confidentiality and IT security. Trust in banking services remains a priority for all consumers who seek, at the same time, to take full advantage of the opportunities offered by the new banking environment. Data analytics can contribute positively to maintaining trust, transparency and security. The use of Big Data in the banking sector is also attractive from a business point of view; it will develop the performance of banks, banking techniques, such as credit analysis, and create new business opportunities.

The use of data analytics represents a competitive advantage that allows banks to run their business more efficiently and at a lower cost. Data analytics will enable banks to adapt to new digital consumer expectations and thus reduce inappropriate marketing expenditure, avoid the development of unnecessary product and services offerings, and focus more effectively on their capacity to innovate for the good of society and its stakeholders.

Multiple Choice Answers

1	**B**	Digitalisation of banks is transforming service delivery from a multichannel approach to an omni-channel approach
2	**B**	The European Banking Federation signed an MOU with Europol to all for the sharing of relevant information on cyber threats
3	**A**	Trust is key to a successful digital single market
4	**A**	Distributed ledgers are commonly referred to as blockchains
5	**B**	The EBF blueprint focuses on the challenges and opportunities in retail banking
6	**B**	The EBF is committed to the digital single market
7	**B**	Banks core values are trust, privacy, security and integrity
8	**C**	Consumers born between 1977 and 1994 are commonly referred to as generation Y
9	**A**	Digitalisation creates new opportunities to engage with consumers differently
10	**B**	The internet security threat report said that 60% of targeted cyber attacks affected SMEs

Chapter 14 – Creativity and What the Future May Hold

Answer 1

The three components of creativity are:

- Expertise
- Creative-thinking skills
- Motivation

Expertise is knowledge; technical; procedural and intellectual.

Creative thinking skills determine how flexibly and imaginatively people approach problems.

An inner passion to solve the problem at hand leads to solutions far more creative than do external rewards, such as money. This component, called intrinsic motivation, is the one that can be most influenced by the work environment.

The first two are more difficult and time consuming to influence than motivation.

The managerial practices that most affect creativity fall into six general categories:

- Challenge
- Freedom
- Resources
- Work-group features
- Supervisory encouragement
- Organisational support

Challenge: managers can match people with jobs that play to their expertise and their skills in creative thinking, and ignite intrinsic motivation.

Freedom: when it comes to granting freedom, the key to creativity is giving people autonomy concerning the means that is, concerning process, but not necessarily the ends.

Resources: the two main resources that affect creativity are time and money. Managers need to allot these resources carefully. Like matching people with the right assignments, deciding how much time and money to give to a team or project is a judgment call that can either support or kill creativity.

Work-group features: if you want to build teams that come up with creative ideas, you must pay careful attention to the design of such teams. That is, you must create mutually supportive groups with a diversity of perspectives and backgrounds.

Supervisory encouragement: to sustain passion, most people need to feel as if their work matters to the organisation or to some important group of people. Otherwise, they might as well do their work at home and for their own personal gain.

Organisational support: encouragement from supervisors fosters creativity, but creativity is truly enhanced when the entire organization supports it. Such support is the job of an organisation's leaders, who must put in place appropriate systems or procedures and emphasise values that make it clear that creative efforts are a top priority.

Answer 2

A futurist's analytical process falls into five general areas:

- **Framing** – understanding the current state of affairs
- **Scanning** – looking for indications of the future

- **Describing** – explaining or reporting on possible futures
- **Visioning** – opening the range of possibilities
- **Planning** – creating/implementing a future direction

Answer 3

There are two types of scanning.

The first is to study the broad trends shaping the world.

Futurists use the acronym STEEP for:

- Society
- Technology
- Economic
- Environmental
- Political

.... to categorise information.

The combination of STEEP trends paints a picture of the direction and the expectations of the future.

Futurists use a very broad view of the world to help understand the interactions between events. The second type of scanning looks for anomalies or unusual events that may provide an indication of change or a solid piece of evidence for an emerging trend, called weak signals.

Most futurists get information from a wide variety of sources including newspapers, books, periodicals, scientific and trade journals, forecasts, interviews with subject matter experts, electronic media, arts and cultural trends.

While most futurists scan broadly for background information, it is most effective when used in combination with a defined, focused framework.

Multiple Choice Answers

1	B	If an organisation is committed to innovation they need to have a high tolerance for risk and failure
2	A	An intrapreneur is an entrepreneur within an already established organisation
3	A	Innovation economics emphasises entrepreneurship, intrapreneurship and innovation
4	B	Sales volumes and time are the two axes in the product life cycle model
5	C	Turnover/sales peak at maturity
6	D	To be creative an idea must be appropriate, useful and actionable
7	B	The carrot and stick method is an example of extrinsic motivation
8	C	Resources is not a function of creativity
9	D	A professional futurist is a person who studies the future in order to help people understand, anticipate, prepare for and gain advantage from coming changes
10	B	An inventor produces ideas

PRACTICE EXAMINATION 1

Question 1

Required

Compare and contrast why RBS and HBOS failed. **(Total marks 40)**

Question 2

Required

(a) What is needed to create a Digital Single Market (DSM) from a banking perspective? **(10 marks)**

(b) What opportunities could the DSM bring for banks and customers? **(5 marks)**

(Total 15 marks)

Question 3

Required

SWOT analysis is a useful tool for auditing the overall strategic position of a business and its environment. It is commonly used in part of strategic planning.

(a) What does the mnemonic SWOT stand for and how can SWOT analysis help management of a business? **(5 marks)**

(b) Provide examples of each of the constituent parts of SWOT. **(10 marks)**

(Total 15 marks)

Question 4

Required

(a) What are quality circles? **(5 marks)**

(b) What are the benefits of quality circles? **(5 marks)**

(c) What are the possible drawbacks of quality circles? **(5 marks)**

(Total 15 marks)

Question 5

Capacity planning aims to balance the capacity of an operation with the demand from customers when demand is either predictable or uncertain.

Required

(a) How do businesses deal with dependent demand and uncertainty? **(5 marks)**

(b) Capacity planning in the short and medium-term has several implications for operational performance. What are they? **(10 marks)**

(Total 15 marks)

PRACTICE EXAMINATION 1
ANSWERS

Answer 1

	RBS	HBOS
Capital	RBS's capital position was far weaker, in terms of its ability to absorb losses, than its published total regulatory capital resources suggested. RBS strategy was of being 'lightly capitalised' relative to its peers.	While regulatory capital ratios remained stable and robust, leverage had increased for HBOS. HBOS had £1 of shareholders' equity supporting every £30 of assets. If account is taken of the significant off balance sheet commitments the true leverage of the firm was significantly higher than 30:1. With a smaller proportion of capital supporting an ever growing balance sheet, the potential impact of a downturn on HBOS had increased.
Liquidity	RBS was excessively dependent on short-term wholesale funding. This reflected the belief that it would always be able to fund itself, a belief which subsequently proved to be mistaken.	The rapid expansion of its balance sheet placed pressure on HBOS's ability to fund itself. HBOS found itself unable meet its liquidity needs from the wholesale market and was facing a withdrawal of customer deposits. The management and Board of HBOS recognised that an over reliance on wholesale funding was a weakness but this was never tackled as a key risk. Indeed, the need for additional funding was viewed as a risk to further asset growth. Higher levels of customer deposits were seen as a way of increasing lending capacity rather than reducing liquidity risk. The closure of the syndication market meant that the corporate division was unable to sell-on significant large exposures that it had agreed to underwrite in full.
Asset quality	There were asset quality concerns and uncertainties arising from aggressive growth. Substantial losses in complex credit trading activities eroded market confidence. Uncertainties about the scale of future loan losses, and potential further credit trading losses, contributed to this loss of confidence.	The Group put itself under pressure to maintain an increasing level of income. As margins declined on all forms of lending, a search for yield pushed it towards more risky propositions. Each of the lending divisions experienced an increase in its risk profile as it sought to grow income levels. This was most evident in the corporate division which became overexposed to the property market.

	RBS	HBOS
		Initially, HBOS was reluctant to accept that loans were going bad, and were reluctant to re-categorise and escalate them to the divisions specialist 'impaired assets' team. As more and more corporate loans deteriorated, the division's impaired assets team became overwhelmed with their sheer volume and was unable to properly re-categorise the loans in a timely fashion. The corporate division proposed levels of provisions did not reflect the declining market conditions and HBOS consistently chose the level of provisions at the least prudent end of the range deemed acceptable by its external auditors.
Acquisition of ABN AMRO	The ABN AMRO acquisition significantly increased RBS's exposure to risky asset categories, reduced an already low capital ratio, and increased potential liquidity strains. RBS's role as the consortium leader and consolidator, created additional potential and perceived risks. RBS's decision to proceed with this acquisition was made on the basis of due diligence which was inadequate in scope and depth.	
Management, governance and culture	Weaknesses evident in: ▪ The bank's management capabilities and style ▪ Its governance arrangements ▪ Checks and balances ▪ Failings for oversight and challenge and in its culture, particularly its attitude to the balance between risk and growth. ▪ The Board's ineffectiveness in challenging the executive, The CEO's management style discouraged robust and effective challenge.	Weaknesses evident in: ▪ Key strategic decisions were taken by the Board which aggravated rather than improved the overall risk profile. ▪ Discussions about the HBOS's strategy and risk appetite tended to focus on performance targets that prioritised growth over the consideration of risk. ▪ The Board played a limited role in the development of the Group business strategy and delegated responsibility for strategic planning to its CEO. ▪ The internal controls within its operating divisions were ineffective and did not keep pace with the rapid growth that these divisions experienced.

RBS	HBOS
▪ The Board designed a CEO remuneration package which focussed on ROE, profitability and growth.	▪ Challenge from Group's internal audit was limited, with some evidence that internal audit reports could be upgraded based on promises from the business to make improvements.
▪ RBS was overly focused on revenue, profit and earnings per share rather than on capital, liquidity and asset quality.	▪ The Board delegated responsibility for the firm's overall systems and controls to the Group CEO.
▪ The Board received adequate information to consider the risks associated with strategy but it was not sufficiently disciplined in questioning and challenging what was presented to it.	▪ The non-executive directors on the Board lacked sufficient experience and knowledge of banking. Of the twelve NEDs only one had a background in banking. This lack of experience hindered the NEDs' ability to provide effective challenge to executive management.
▪ Risk management information enabled the Board adequately to monitor and mitigate all the risks across the group but it was not sufficiently forward-looking to give early warning of emerging risks.	▪ The lack of experience and knowledge of banking amongst the NEDs was compounded by similar lack of banking experience within the executive management team.

Summary

Both banks failed for very similar reasons, albeit there were idiosyncrasies for each individual bank. Common areas of failure included the following:

Growth strategies: both banks embarked on strategies based on achieving aggressive growth targets and gaining market share.

Focus on earnings: both boards were overly focused on revenue, profit and earnings per share rather than on capital, liquidity and asset quality.

Capital: both banks were lightly capitalised and highly leveraged.

Liquidity: both became excessively dependent on wholesale funding. When the wholesale funding markets closed both were badly exposed and ran out of liquidity. Both had to receive government support to continue trading.

Asset quality: both had asset quality concerns and uncertainties arising from aggressive growth strategies.

HBOS were reluctant to accept their loans were going bad, and their impaired asset team became overwhelmed. In HBOS the provisioning strategy was at the least prudent end deemed to be acceptable by their external auditors.

Complexity and credit trading: RBS had substantial losses in complex credit trading activities which eroded market confidence. Uncertainties about the scale of future loan losses, and potential further credit trading losses, contributed to this loss of confidence. The ABN AMRO acquisition significantly increased RBS's exposure to risky asset categories, reduced an already low capital ratio, and increased potential liquidity strains. RBS's decision to proceed with this acquisition was made on the basis of due diligence which was inadequate in scope and depth.

HBOS were less exposed to complex trading activities, instead they were over exposed to the property market (especially commercial property), which was a deliberate strategy aimed at 'lending through the cycle'. The corporate division willingly took on other banks exposures that were high risk and badly priced.

Risk and control: both banks had access to adequate risk information but were insufficiently disciplined to challenge what was presented to them.

This was particularly evident in HBOS where the NEDs and the executive management had little banking experience.

Corporate governance (oversight and challenge): both boards delegated too much responsibility to their respective CEOs and both CEOs were insufficiently challenged by their respective boards.

In short, corporate governance in both banks failed, as did they.

Answer 2

Creating a digital single market that responds to the reality of the banking market is one of the priorities of the European Banking Federation, which is actively committed to the future of banks.

Banks channel savings to investments to ensure economic activity and growth and provide essential services in a secure and reliable way for their customers, consumers and corporates alike. They embrace the digital innovation opportunity, accelerating the rethinking of their traditional business model, proposing innovative products/apps, engaging in FinTech partnerships, and financing innovative starts-ups. Banks perform indispensable functions within the economy and in this way strengthen EU competitiveness and stimulate investment for growth and job creation.

The banking sector supports a competitive and innovative EU digital single market which safeguards existing consumer protection, trust and security. In the banks' view, there is not necessarily a conflict between innovation and security. The key to a successful digital single market is trust. To protect consumers and their data within a new digital economy, companies offering services similar to those of banks, and facing comparable risks, should be subject to appropriate and equivalent rules. This implies the need to find the proper balance between competition, innovation, security, privacy, and consumer protection. Strengthening cooperation and raising the awareness of EU citizens on the growing threats from cyber crime is crucial. Making digital finance secure and building trust should be a concern for all, including public and private sectors.

The EBF Blueprint proposes recommendations on which to build a proper framework for a workable digital single market (DSM) in particular on key issues:

- Better access to banking products and services
- Data value chain/big data
- Digital payments (mobile/instant and e-invoicing)
- Cyber security
- Crypto-technologies
- E-identification/e-signature
- Digital skills (competence/talent recruitment and education)
- Removing regulatory inconsistencies.

Banks have started to make significant investments to improve the access of their customers to their new digital banking products and services. In particular, the development of sophisticated technologies such as biometric, audio, voice and image recognition software, data analytics and high-performance computing infrastructure. Today, banks provide customised deals at select stores through mobile apps, 24 hours, 7 days a week, account balance control, new concept stores or remote adviser systems connecting financial experts to customers from their branch or a mobile device via high quality video which allows financial planning, problem resolution and assistance/advice.

These new innovative banking solutions let banks provide a tailor-made customer experience which facilitates a faster access to banking products and services. More importantly, they ease the interaction between banks and their customers who are able to search further and faster for the best deals/value when and how it suits them. Now instead of having numerous passwords or log-ins, a number of banks propose biometric security solutions to customers, such as facial, fingerprint or voice recognition tools. The contact customers have with a bank also goes through new channels such as social media (for example Twitter, Facebook) or secure instant messaging platforms similar to Viber or WhatsApp.

New banking technology also has a positive impact on the management of customer finance, especially via budgeting programmes developed by banks or through automated advice. It further contributes to helping consumers avoid financial mistakes such as overlooking the payment of bills and running into overdraft. This potentially prevents customers from being charged penalty fees.

Answer 3

SWOT stands for:

Strengths
Weaknesses
Opportunities
Threats.

That is:

- Internal strengths
- Internal weaknesses
- Opportunities in the external environment
- Threats in the external environment.

SWOT can help management in a business discover:

- What the business does better than the competition
- What competitors do better than the business
- Whether the business is making the most of the opportunities available
- How the business should respond to changes in its external environment.

Strategy should be devised around strengths and opportunities. It is concerned with converting weaknesses into strengths and strengths into opportunities. It should look to how best to turn threats into opportunities.

Completing a SWOT relies on a good level of objectivity, and critiquing the content on a simple 'so what' basis is a useful exercise. The challenge is to avoid generalities and think incisively about the components of the boxes. The acid test is usually 'relevance to customers'; for example a strength that is of no real interest to the marketplace is not really a strength. Strengths must either:

- Increase sales
- Increase margins.

If it does not achieve either of these, it is not a strength. Strengths help to build up competitive advantage and serve as a cornerstone of strategy. Strengths should be protected and built upon.

Examples of strengths could include:

- High market share
- Economies of scale
- High quality
- Financial resources
- Technology
- Brand
- Skills
- R&D

Weaknesses are a source of competitive disadvantage, such as things the business lacks or does poorly that places a business at a disadvantage or that may hinder or constrain the business in achieving its objectives. Management should seek ways to reduce or eliminate weaknesses before they are exploited further by the competition. Weakness should be seen as areas for improvement.

Examples of weaknesses could include:

- Low market share
- Low productivity
- Poor quality
- Inadequate financial resources
- Outdated technology
- Weak brand
- Poor skills
- Inadequate R&D.

An opportunity is any feature of the external environment that creates positive potential for the business to achieve its objectives.

Examples of opportunities could include:

- Technical innovation
- New demand
- Market growth
- Demographic changes
- Social or lifestyle changes
- Government spending programmes
- Higher economic growth
- Trade liberalisation
- Deregulation.

Threats are any external development that may hinder or prevent the business from achieving its objectives.

Possible sources of business threats include:

- New entrants
- New substitute products
- Changes in consumer demand/taste
- Demographic changes
- Consolidation along the supply chain
- New regulation
- Economic down turn
- Completive price pressures.

Answer 4

Ishikawa stressed the importance of people and participation to improve quality. He is often credited with the idea of quality circles, and their use to achieve participation and overcome resistance to quality initiatives.

A typical quality circle comprises employees from many levels of the organisation who meet regularly. The frequency of meetings varies across organisations, for example every three months. Suggestions are encouraged regarding how the product or service produced could be made better, and how processes and working practices could be improved. Members are encouraged to analyse issues in a logical way. Wider issues may also be discussed, as it is recognised that the complete working environment will affect quality levels. In some organisations this has led to quality circles having input on issues such as health and safety, employee benefits and bonuses, and training and education programmes.

An organisation can encourage the use of quality circles by:

- Rewarding the circle for suggestions that are implemented (e.g. a share of any savings made).

- Providing a budget and support to run quality circles.

- Ensuring management is supportive and prepared to act on useful suggestions from the circle.

- Providing an explanation as to why suggestions not implemented were rejected.

- Management asking the circle for suggestions and comments on specific issues and problems. facing the company, without anticipating the outcomes.

The benefits of quality circles include:

- Employee involvement and participation improves morale.
- Practical improvements/solutions are likely as workers know the processes involved.
- Organisational unity is fostered as the circle includes all levels.
- Suggestions can result in valuable savings.
- A 'culture' of quality is fostered.

The possible drawbacks of quality circles include:

- Employee 'power' is hard to control.
- The scope of influence can become very wide.
- Rejected suggestions may cause resentment.
- Business practicalities (e.g. cost) may not be fully understood.

The concept of quality circles has expanded to now include groups drawn from separate organisations but with a common interest, such as other participants in the value chain.

Answer 5

One important operational management task within an organisation is balancing the amount it is able to produce (capacity) with the amount it is able to sell (demand).

Uncertainties in capacity could be caused by a number of factors, for example the shortage or a delay in the supply of a resource. Uncertainties in demand are often due to the unpredictable nature of customers and potential customers. Dealing with uncertainty requires flexibility in planning and control.

Dependent demand relates to demand that is predictable because it is based on factors that are known. Dependent demand occurs often in manufacturing, where the demand for raw materials and components can be predicted from the demand for the main product.

Many organisations and/or operations within organisations are not able to predict demand as easily. They have to make capacity decisions based on experience and judgement about the likely level of demand.

Capacity planning aims to balance the capacity of an operation with the demand from customers. The objective is to maximise both profits and customer satisfaction.

Planning and controlling capacity involves:

- Planning the normal capacity of the operation
- Reacting to changes in demand.

Capacity planning in the short and medium-term has several implications for operational performance.

Cost: costs are affected by planned capacity. When the capacity of an operation exceeds demand, there will be under-utilised resources and costs will be higher than if capacity were more closely matched to demand.

Revenue: revenues could also be affected by the capacity of an operation. If demand exceeds the capacity of an operation to meet it, revenues will be forgone that could otherwise have been earned.

Quality: the quality of an operation could be affected by capacity planning. For example, if an operation varies its capacity by using part-time or temporary staff, the quality of the product or service might be compromised.

Speed of response to demand: the speed of response to demand can be improved either by building up finished goods inventories (which has a cost) or by providing sufficient capacity to avoid customers having to queue or to wait (which also has a cost).

Dependability of supply: the closer an operation works to its capacity limit, the less easily it will be able to cope with unexpected disruptions to the work flow. Supply will therefore be less dependable.

Flexibility: the flexibility of an operation, and in particular its ability to vary the volume of output it can produce, will be improved by having surplus capacity. An operation working at or close to its capacity limit is much less flexible.

BPP
LEARNING MEDIA

PRACTICE EXAMINATION 2

Question 1

Bradford & Bingley

Bradford & Bingley plc had a history stretching back to 1851, the year in which both the Bradford Equitable Building Society and the Bingley Building Society were established. The two societies merged in 1964 and operated as the Bradford & Bingley Building Society until the year 2000 when Bradford & Bingley's members voted to demutualise the society and form a public limited company. Bradford & Bingley's Annual Report in the year prior to demutualisation, 1999, reported that Bradford & Bingley had a loan book of £18.4 billion and retail savings balances amounting to £15.5 billion.

It was from this robust platform that the demutualisation of the building society received overwhelming support from its members: 94% of voting investors and 89% of voting borrower members supported the resolution. By June 2008, Bradford & Bingley's residential loan book stood at £41.3 billion while customer deposits amounted to £24.5 billion.

Bradford & Bingley's expansion was aided by a number of acquisitions which began prior to demutualisation. These included the acquisition of Mortgage Express in 1997, John Charcol Holding Ltd, a mortgage broker with a growing internet mortgage broking arm in 2000 and the Independent Financial Advisor company Aitchison & Colegrave Group Ltd in 2003.

The acquisition of Mortgage Express was a definitive act by Bradford & Bingley's board. Mortgage Express was a specialist mortgage lender focusing on lending to the self-employed using self-certification mortgages. After that acquisition, Bradford & Bingley began rapidly to expand this area of its business, using its Mortgage Express arm to focus on self-certification, buy-to-let and providing 100% plus (loan to value) mortgages. Upon acquisition, Mortgage Express accounted for 4% of total Bradford & Bingley lending; after just a year, in 1998, this figure had risen to 15% of new loans; and by 2000 it was 40%.

A second element to Bradford & Bingley's growth was a series of deals with the US company General Motors Acceptance Corporation (GMAC). The first of these, announced in 2002, committed Bradford & Bingley to acquiring a mixed loan portfolio of £650m buy-to-let, self-certified and standard loans from GMAC. This deal was followed by a flurry of loan acquisitions in 2003: £470m was taken on from GMAC in March; £106m in October; £450m in November; and a three year agreement covering £1.4 billion of loans was signed in December 2003.

A second three year agreement was signed in 2006. Bradford & Bingley continued to implement this agreement after it fell into public ownership. The last tranche of loans was handed over from GMAC to the rump of Bradford & Bingley in public ownership on 27 February 2009. This committed Bradford & Bingley to purchasing a minimum of £350m of UK mortgage assets per quarter for three years.

In total, Bradford & Bingley had taken on £6.5 billion of self-certified and buy-to-let UK mortgages from GMAC by the time it was nationalised. At the time of this first GMAC deal the then Group Chief Executive of Bradford & Bingley, Christopher Rodrigues, argued that such acquisitions would 'improve return on equity for our shareholders'.

The current Chairman, Richard Pym said that one of the reasons for buying loans from GMAC was that its network of mortgage intermediaries differed slightly from that of Bradford & Bingley. Mr Pym admitted that, 'with the benefit of hindsight, the inflexibility that was built in to the GMAC contract did not allow us the flexibility that we would otherwise have liked as the market deteriorated'. He identified the principal problem as the fact that 'the underwriting criteria that was written into the contract in December 2006, meant that when credit conditions deteriorated there was no ability to change the underwriting criteria for the loans'.

In defence of the Board's decision to pursue the GMAC contract, Mr Pym said that when the restrictive contract was signed, they simply found it 'difficult to envisage the economic circumstances which later emerged'. He defended his predecessors, arguing that at 'that point there was probably no real reason why you would do that because you were not expecting the highly adverse situation that we have now'. Mr Pym also acknowledged, the default rate on GMAC mortgages was 'marginally higher' than the default rate of Bradford & Bingley's own mortgages.

Mr Pym also confirmed that Bradford & Bingley's business was 60% buy-to-let and 20% self-certified and that the value of buy-to-let mortgages alone on Bradford & Bingley's book was £24 billion, a figure which represented 20% of the UK buy-to-let market. In Mr Pym's view, this business model had left Bradford & Bingley materially more exposed than other mortgage lenders. He confirmed that 'the total arrears in the business including repossessions were 2.48% at the end of June, which is above the level of the Council of Mortgage Lenders overall, and at the end of September it was over 3%'. In defending this business model, Mr Pym argued that 'the strategic analysis was done that these mortgages were paying a higher interest rate, a higher spread over base rate' and was attractive even when the return was adjusted for risk. He went on to admit that 'obviously that assessment has not turned out to be the case'.

The Bradford & Bingley argued that its down fall was caused by difficulties in obtaining both wholesale and retail funding The gap in the size of the increase in retail deposits (59%) relative to that in loans (124%) suggests that Bradford & Bingley, in common with many other financial Institutions, funded much of this growth via the wholesale markets. The availability of wholesale funding reduced and the cost of both retail and wholesale funding increased. The market value of some of the bank's treasury assets reduced. Mortgage arrears increased and customers found it more difficult to secure mortgages elsewhere, increasing Bradford & Bingley's funding needs.

These adverse conditions necessitated a drive to raise capital and in May 2008 Bradford & Bingley announced a rights issue. It was during this capital-raising process that the deterioration in Bradford & Bingley's trading outlook for the year became apparent.

Through June and July 2008 Bradford & Bingley had its credit rating cut by the major ratings agencies which, it reported, led to withdrawals of wholesale and retail deposits. When the collapse came for Bradford & Bingley it was sudden and dramatic. In the week commencing 22 September 2008, in a single 24 hour period, the company had £90m withdrawn from its branches. The position on the Wednesday was that the bank had an outflow of funds from the branches and from online of £12 million. On the Thursday they lost a further £26 million. On the Friday, following further media reporting, they lost around £90 million and by lunchtime on the Saturday had an outflow of around £200 million from branches and online. It was that which forced the authorities to act.

Mr Pym estimated that , based on an assumed 25% fall in house prices, Bradford & Bingley's losses would fall in the £600m–800m range but could offer no guarantees that even these estimates would not be exceeded.

After 149 years as a mutual, Bradford & Bingley's life as a plc lasted a little over eight years, ending on 29 September 2008 when the Chancellor announced that, under the Banking Supervisions (Special Provisions) Act 2008, Bradford & Bingley's retail deposit business and branch networks would be transferred to Abbey with the remainder of the business being taken into public ownership.

Required

Summarise why Bradford & Bingley failed.   **(40 marks)**

Question 2   Chapter 14

Required

(a)   What role does motivation play in creativity? → Intrinsic Extrinsic   **(5 marks)**
(b)   What kind of managerial practices can stimulate creativity?   **(10 marks)**
        L   CFR WOSO   **(Total 15 marks)**

Question 3

Operational structures can be described as being tall or flat.

Chapter 5

Required

(a)   Explain what is meant by tall and flat structures.   **(5 marks)**
(b)   List the advantages and disadvantages of each type of structure.   **(10 marks)**
(Total 15 marks)

Question 4

Required

(a)   Describe what control systems are.   **(5 marks)**
(b)   Discuss the limitations of control systems and how these limitations could be mitigated.
(10 marks)
(Total 15 marks)

Question 5

Chapter 8

Required

(a)   What are the ISO 9000 quality standards?   **(10 marks)**
(b)   What are the key benefits of ISO 9000?   **(5 marks)**
(Total 15 marks)

PRACTICE EXAMINATION 2
ANSWERS

Answer 1

The failure of Bradford & Bingley was similar, in part, to the reasons why RBS and HBOS failed.

Capital

A weak capital position in terms of its ability to absorb losses. As a consequence of rapid growth Bradford & Bingley leveraged its balance sheet to a point where it was unsustainable. In 1999 the bank funded its loan book from retail savings (84%). In 2008 this had fallen to 59%, prior to the catastrophic outflow of retail deposits, which in one week saw deposits of £418m, leave the company. The board undertook to improve its capital position by a rights issue but events happened so quickly, it was unable to successfully close out the rights issue. With a smaller proportion of capital supporting its ever growing balance sheet, the potential impact on a downturn in the economy with house prices falling had increased significantly.

Liquidity

As with many banks Bradford & Bingley became, in time, over exposed and reliant upon the wholesale funding market. When the wholesale markets froze, the costs of funding increased and the market value of some of the bank's treasury assets reduced. Mortgage arrears increased and its customers found it increasingly difficult to secure mortgages elsewhere because other banks and financial institutions were unwilling to take on buy to let business, 100% mortgages and self certified mortgages.

Due to the raid expansion of its balance sheet Bradford & Bingley became unable to fund itself. It was unable to meet its liquidity needs from the markets and experienced a substantial withdrawal of customer deposits.

Asset quality

There was evidence of asset quality concerns arising from excessive growth. The GMAC business was acknowledged to be at a higher rate than Bradford & Bingley's own default rate. Total arrears were running at over 3%, a level that exceeded the level of the Council of Mortgage Lenders overall.

It is noted that the GMAC business were paying a higher rates of interest which reflected the higher risk of these mortgages. This suggests risk was being underpriced.

Management and corporate governance

Raid growth was poorly managed. Huge volumes of debt were taken on from the GMAC business as it sought to become the largest mortgage provider in the UK.

The GMAC business, with hindsight, was taken on without adequate due diligence. The deal committed to take on future amounts of debt (even after its collapse). The inflexibly built into the GMAC contract meant that there was no ability to change underwriting criteria in the event of an economic downturn. In 2006 when the first contract was signed, the board did not foresee what affect a downturn would have on the business, presuming that house prices and more new business would always increase.

The board subjected the business to strategic risk as it sought to become to become the UK's market leader in the high risk buy-to-let and self certified market and 100% mortgages.

The board became over focused on revenues and return on capital rather than capital, liquidity and asset quality and was not sufficiently forward looking to give early warning signs of emerging risks, including the speed at which customers deposits could flow out of the business.

The regulatory authorities also failed to recognise strategic risks and the impact this would have on the business.

Answer 2

Creativity refers to the way people think, and how inventively they approach problems. Indeed, thinking imaginatively is one part of creativity, but two others are also essential, expertise and motivation.

Expertise encompasses everything that a person knows and can do in the broad domain of his or her work. Creative thinking refers to how people approach problems and solutions, their capacity to put existing ideas together in new combinations. The skill itself depends quite a bit on personality as well as on how a person thinks and works. Expertise and creative thinking are an individual's raw materials, his or her natural resources. But a third factor, motivation, determines what people will actually do.

People can have outstanding educational credentials and a great facility in generating new perspectives to old problems but if they lack the motivation to do a particular job, they simply won't do it and their expertise and creative thinking will either go untapped or will be applied to something else.

There are two types of motivation, extrinsic and intrinsic, the latter being far more essential for creativity.

Extrinsic motivation comes from outside a person, whether the motivation is a carrot or a stick. This could translate it self as a promise of reward (usually financial) or the threat of dismissal or demotion in the event of failure. This sort of motivation makes the person do their job in order to get something desirable or avoid something painful.

Money by itself does not make employees passionate about their jobs. A cash reward can not magically prompt people to find their work interesting if in their hearts they feel it is dull. Money does not necessarily stop people from being creative, but in many situations, it does not really help.

Passion and interest, a person's internal desire to do something, is what intrinsic motivation is all about. For instance, a personal sense of challenge, or a drive to crack a problem that no one else has been able to solve. When people are intrinsically motivated, they engage in their work for the challenge and enjoyment of it. The work itself is motivating.

Intrinsic motivation can be increased considerably by even subtle changes in an organisation's environment. That is not to say that managers should give up on improving expertise and creative-thinking skills. But when it comes to pulling levers, they should know that those that affect intrinsic motivation will yield more immediate results.

Managerial practices that affect creativity fall into six categories:

1   Challenge
2   Freedom
3   Resources
4   Work-group features
5   Supervisory encouragement
6   Organisational support.

Challenge

Of all the things managers can do to stimulate creativity, perhaps the most efficacious is the deceptively simple task of matching people with the right assignments. Managers can match people with jobs that play to their expertise and their skills in creative thinking, and ignite intrinsic motivation. Perfect matches stretch employees' abilities. The amount of stretch, however, is crucial; not so little that they feel bored but not so much that they feel overwhelmed and threatened by a loss of control. Making a good match requires that managers possess rich and detailed information about their employees and the available assignments.

Freedom

When it comes to granting freedom, the key to creativity is giving people autonomy concerning the means to the process, but not necessarily the ends. People will be more creative if you give them freedom to decide how to climb a particular mountain. You needn't let them choose which mountain to climb. In fact, clearly specified strategic goals often enhance people's creativity. Creativity thrives when managers let people decide how to climb a mountain; they needn't, however, let employees choose which one.

Autonomy around process fosters creativity because giving people freedom in how they approach their work also heightens their intrinsic motivation and sense of ownership. Freedom about process also allows people to approach problems in ways that make the most of their expertise and their creative-thinking skills. The task may end up being a stretch for them, but they can use their strengths to meet the challenge.

Resources

The two main resources that affect creativity are time and money. Managers need to allot these resources carefully. Like matching people with the right assignments, deciding how much time and money to give to a team or project is a judgment call that can either support or kill creativity.

Work-group features

If you want to build teams that come up with creative ideas, you must pay careful attention to the design of such teams. That is, you must create mutually supportive groups with a diversity of perspectives and backgrounds. When teams comprise people with various intellectual foundations and approaches to work that are different, expertise and creative thinking styles and ideas often combine and combust in exciting and useful ways.

Supervisory encouragement

Most managers are extremely busy. They are under pressure for results. It is therefore easy for them to allow praise for creative efforts, not just creative successes but unsuccessful efforts, to, fall by the wayside. One simple step managers can take to foster creativity is to not let that happen. The connection to intrinsic motivation here is clear. Certainly, people can find their work interesting or exciting without a cheering section, for some period of time. But to sustain such passion, most people need to feel as if their work matters to the organisation or to some important group of people. Otherwise, they might as well do their work at home and for their own personal gain.

Managers in successful, creative organisations freely and generously recognise creative work by individuals and teams, often before the ultimate commercial impact of those efforts is known.

Another way managers can support creativity is to serve as role models, persevering through tough problems as well as encouraging collaboration and communication within the team. Such behaviour enhances all three components of the creative process, and it has the added virtue of being a high-impact practice that a single manager can take on his or her own. It is better still when all managers in an organisation serve as role models for the attitudes and behaviours that encourage and nurture creativity.

Organisational support

Encouragement from supervisors fosters creativity, but creativity is truly enhanced when the entire organisation supports it. Such support is the job of an organisation's leaders, who must put in place appropriate systems or procedures and emphasise values that make it clear that creative efforts are a top priority.

An organisation's leaders can support creativity by mandating information sharing and collaboration and by ensuring that political problems do not emerge and fester. Information sharing and collaboration support all three components of creativity. Take expertise. The more often people exchange ideas and data by working together, the more knowledge they will have.

Answer 3

Recent trends have been towards delayering organisations of levels of management. In other words, tall organisations (with many management levels and narrow spans of control) are turning into flat organisations (with fewer management levels and wider spans of control) as a result of technological changes and the granting of more decision-making power to front line employees.

The span of control concept has implications for the length of the chain of command from the most senior to the most junior.

- A tall organisation is one which, in relation to its size, has a large number of levels of management hierarchy. This implies a narrow span of control.

- A flat organisation is one which, in relation to its size, has a small number of hierarchical levels. This implies a wide span of control.

The advantages and disadvantages of these organisational forms can be summarised as follows.

Tall organisations

Advantages

- Narrow control spans

- Small groups enable team members to participate in decisions

- A large number of steps on the promotional ladders- assists management training and career planning

Disadvantages

- Inhibits delegation
- Rigid supervision can be imposed, blocking initiative
- The same work passes through too many hands
- Increases administration and overhead costs
- Slow decision making and responses, as the strategic apex is further away

Flat organisations

Advantages

- More opportunity for delegation
- Relatively cheap
- In theory, speeds up communication between strategic apex and operating core

Disadvantages

- Requires that jobs can be delegated. Managers may only get a superficial idea of what goes on. If they are overworked they are more likely to be involved in crisis management

- Sacrifices control

- Middle managers are often necessary to convert the grand vision of the strategic apex into operational terms

Answer 4

Information systems can be used to monitor and control the outcomes of plans and once a plan is implemented, its actual performance must be controlled. Information is required to assess whether it is proceeding as expected or whether there is some unexpected deviation from the plan. It may consequently be necessary to take some form of corrective action. Control systems must be dynamic and not static. This implies that there must be a flow of information to ensure that managers may take decisions not only to deal with variances in performance of the system but also to pre-empt future issues and problems.

Control systems (MIS) convert data from mainly internal sources into information for example summary reports, exception reports. This information enables managers to make timely and effective decisions for planning and directing and controlling the activities for which they are responsible.

Control systems have the following characteristics:

- Support structured decisions at operational and management control levels
- Designed to report on existing operations
- Have little analytical capability
- Relatively inflexible
- Have an internal focus

Limitations of internal control systems

Any internal control system can only provide the directors with reasonable assurance that their objectives are reached, because of inherent limitations of internal controls, such as:

- The requirement that the cost of an internal control is not disproportionate to the potential loss which may result from its absence. A cost/benefit analysis may need to be undertaken.

- The tendency for most systematic internal controls to be directed at routine transactions rather than non-routine transactions. A system should be set up that takes non-routine transactions into account.

- The potential for human error due to carelessness, distraction, mistakes of judgement and the misunderstanding of instructions. Training procedures and recruitment of staff that have the capabilities and qualifications necessary to carry out responsibilities properly should help alleviate this limitation.

- The possibility of circumvention of internal controls through collusion with parties outside or inside the entity. This is a difficult situation to control, as a determined fraudster who is colluding with external parties may be difficult to detect, but internal and external audit procedures may have a reasonable chance of detecting such practices.

- The possibility that a person responsible for exercising an internal control could abuse that responsibility by overriding an internal control. The vigilance of other members of staff and the willingness to report such behaviour must be encouraged.

- The possibility that procedures may become inadequate due to changes in conditions or that compliance with procedures may deteriorate over time. An internal audit department should be able to verify that the control system is working and to review the system to ensure that it is still appropriate for current circumstances.

Answer 5

The ISO 9000 standards provide guidance and tools for companies and organisations who want to ensure that their products and services consistently meet customer's requirements, and that quality is consistently improved.

The ISO 9000 family addresses various aspects of quality management. Standards include:

- ISO 9001:2015 – sets out the requirements of a quality management system

- ISO 9000:2015 – covers the basic concepts and language

- ISO 9004:2009 – focuses on how to make a quality management system more efficient and effective

- ISO 19011:2011 – sets out guidance on internal and external audits of quality management systems.

It has become an international reference for quality requirements in business-to-business dealings and can be applied to any organisation, irrespective of its size and industry.

It focuses on quality management; what the organisation does to enhance customer satisfaction by meeting customer requirements and continually improving its performance in this area'.

This standard is based on a number of quality management principles including:

- A strong customer focus
- The motivation and implications for top management
- The process approach
- Continual improvement.

Using ISO 9001:2015 helps ensure that customers get consistent, good quality products and services, which in turn brings many business benefits.

The seven quality management principles are:

1 Customer focus
2 Leadership
3 Engagement of people
4 Process approach
5 Improvement
6 Evidence-based decision making
7 Relationship management.

These principles are not listed in priority order. The relative importance of each principle will vary from organisation to organisation and can be expected to change over time.

ISO 9000 can help an organisation to:

- Recognise direct and indirect customers as those who receive value from the organisation

- Understand customers' current and future needs and expectations

- Link the organisation's objectives to customer needs and expectations

- Communicate customer needs and expectations throughout the organisation

- Plan, design, develop, produce, deliver and support goods and services to meet customer needs and expectations

- Measure and monitor customer satisfaction and take appropriate actions

Key benefits of ISO 9000:

- Increased customer value

- Increased customer satisfaction

- Improved customer loyalty

- Enhanced repeat business

- Enhanced reputation of the organisation

- Expanded customer base

- Increased revenue and market share

- Determine and take actions on interested parties' needs and expectations that can affect customer satisfaction

- Actively manage relationships with customers to achieve sustained success.

PRACTICE EXAMINATION 3

Question 1

Required

Describe the Basel Accords and explain the differences between them. Explain the Basel approach operational risk.

(a)	Basel I	**(5 marks)**
(b)	Basel II	**(15 marks)**
(c)	Basel III	**(15 marks)**
(d)	Operational risk	**(5 marks)**

(Total 40 marks)

Question 2

Required

Explain the differences between quality control and quality assurance. **(15 marks)**

(Total 15 marks)

Question 3

Required

(a)	What are the aims of government regulation?	**(10 marks)**
(b)	What role does the Financial Policy Committee (FPC) take in regulation?	**(5 marks)**

(Total 15 marks)

Question 4

Required

(a) Define service quality. **(1 mark)**

(b) Describe the major factors that shape customer expectations and provide examples for each. **(9 marks)**

(c) Explain how service quality factors can be classified, again, provide examples. **(5 marks)**

(Total 15 marks)

Question 5

For supply chains and networks to operate successfully information must flow smoothly between all participating organisations. One way of analysing and representing information flows is with the use of process maps.

Required

(a)	What are process maps?	**(5 marks)**
(b)	Why are process maps important and what are the benefits of process mapping?	**(10 marks)**

(Total 15 marks)

PRACTICE EXAMINATION 3
ANSWERS

Answer 1

In 1988, the Basel Committee on Banking Supervision (BCBS) published the first international capital framework for banks, entitled International Convergence of Capital Measurement and Capital Standards (Basel I Accord). The purpose of that regime was to make capital requirements more risk sensitive and commensurate with the degree of risk inherent in banks' balance sheets.

This regime required banks to hold minimum levels of capital equal to 8% of risk-weighted balance sheets assets. The risk weights assigned to various asset classes were designed to reflect the degree of uncertainty surrounding the payoff of broad asset classes and, in that sense, reflected their intrinsic credit risk. While Basel I was generally perceived as a step forward in making capital requirements more risk sensitive, the Financial services Authority (FSA) required additional capital charges to compensate for several recognised shortfalls. The Basel I regime, in particular, did not consider a number of other key risks, including:

- Interest rate
- Legal
- Reputational
- Operational risks

For that reason, the FSA set individual capital guidance, also known as trigger ratios, based on firm-specific reviews and judgments about, among other things, evolving market conditions as well as the quality of risk management and banks' systems and controls. Such limitations were the catalyst for a new accord to replace Basel I.

Basel II was the second of the Basel Accords, which were recommendations on banking laws and regulations. Basel II, initially published in June 2004, was intended to create an international standard for banking regulators to control how much capital banks need to put aside to guard against the types of financial and operational risks banks face. Advocates of Basel II believed that such an international standard could help protect the international financial system from the types of problems that might arise should a major bank or a series of banks collapse. Basel II attempted to accomplish this by setting up risk and capital management requirements designed to ensure that a bank had adequate capital for the risk it exposed itself to through its lending and investment practices. Generally speaking, these rules mean that the greater risk to which the bank is exposed, the greater the amount of capital the bank needs to hold to safeguard its solvency and overall economic stability.

There were four main components to the framework:

1. It was more sensitive to the risks that banks face.

2. The framework included an explicit measure for operational risk and included more risk sensitive risk weightings against credit risk.

3. It reflected improvements in bank's risk-management practices, for example the internal ratings based approach (IRB) allowing banks to rely to a certain extent on their own estimates of credit risk.

4. It provided incentives for banks to improve their risk management practices, with more risk-sensitive risk weightings as banks adopted more sophisticated approaches to risk management.

Basel II introduced the concept of three pillars.

- **Pillar 1**: minimum capital requirements – a quantification of the risks arising from banks' credit, trading and other businesses.

- **Pillar 2**: supervisory review – the establishment of a strong constructive dialogue between a bank and the regulator on the risks, risk management and capital requirements of the bank.

- **Pillar 3**: market discipline – robust requirements on public disclosure intended to give the market a stronger role in ensuring that banks held an appropriate level of capital.

Basel II intended to promote a more forward-looking approach to capital supervision, and one that encouraged banks to identify the risks they may face, both at the present moment and in the future, and to develop or improve their ability to manage those risks. It established an explicit capital charge for a bank's exposures to the risk of operational risk losses caused by failures in systems, processes, or staff or those that are caused by external events, such as natural disasters. Banks would choose their own approaches for measuring their exposures to operational risk that they and their supervisors agreed reflected the quality and sophistication of their internal controls over a particular risk area. By aligning capital charges more closely to a bank's own measures of its exposures to credit and operational risk, Basel II encouraged banks to refine those measures. It also provided explicit incentives in the form of lower capital requirements for banks to adopt more comprehensive and accurate measures of risk as well as more effective processes for controlling their exposures to risk.

Pillar 2 of the Basel II capital framework recognised the necessity of exercising effective supervisory review of banks' internal assessments of their overall risks to ensure that bank management was exercising sound judgement and had set aside adequate capital for these risks. Regulators would evaluate the activities and risk profiles of individual banks to determine whether those organisations should hold higher levels of capital than the minimum requirements in Pillar 1 would specify and to see whether there was any need for remedial actions.

The Basel Committee expected that, when regulators engaged banks in a dialogue about their internal processes for measuring and managing their risks, they would help to create implicit incentives for organisations to develop sound control structures and to improve those processes. Supervisors would review the processes and strategies and if they identified weaknesses or deficiencies, would take appropriate prudential measures, including the setting of a higher capital requirement. A central assumption of Basel II was that the formulation of the internal capital adequacy assessment process would be the duty and responsibility of the institution itself. Responsibility for the internal capital adequacy assessment process lay with the institution's own board of directors and senior management, while the supervisory authority's fundamental task was to assess whether the board and senior management of the institution had complied with their responsibility in an adequate manner. If not, the institution would have to take appropriate action.

Pillar 3 leveraged the ability of market discipline to motivate prudent management by enhancing the degree of transparency in banks' public reporting. It set out the public disclosures that banks must make that provide greater insight into the adequacy of their capitalisation. The Basel Committee believed that, when marketplace participants had a sufficient understanding of a bank's activities and the controls it has in place to manage its exposures, they would be better able to distinguish between banking organisations so that they could reward those that manage their risks prudently and penalise those that did not.

Following the global financial crisis the G20 leaders endorsed a new Basel III in 2010. It introduced new regulations which included:

- Tighter definitions of common equity, with a requirement for banks to hold 4.5% by January 2015 (compared with 2.0% previously), then a further capital conservation buffer of 2.5% to withstand future periods of stress, totalling 7%.

- A framework for counter-cyclical capital buffers, with banks having a capital ratio below 2.5% facing restrictions on dividends, buybacks and bonuses.

- Measures to limit counterparty credit risk.

- Short and medium-term quantitative liquidity ratios.

- The introduction of an internationally harmonised leverage ratio, acting as a backstop to risk-based capital measures.

The new capital standards require banks the whole world over to have larger buffers of capital through which to absorb losses. Under this new regime banks will hold about three times as much equity as they used to under the old one. In some places the cushion could be even greater and higher levels of capital mean lower returns on equity. This is leaving the regulators with a difficult conundrum to balance.

For example, many of Europe's banks need to bolster their capital buffers but few will be able to entice investors since they promise such low returns. The danger is that some banks would struggle to generate the capital they need from profits. Many banks therefore might seek therefore simply to reduce the size of their loan books instead. This may have the effect of preventing credit from being granted to companies and households which would impact on the broader economy and diminish growth within economies.

Much of Basel III's new requirements addresses the management of liquidity risk trying to ensure the banks are better at managing liquidity risk in the future. This is to be achieved by the introduction of a leverage ratio together with short and medium-term quantitative liquidity ratios. The two measures addressing liquidity management are known as the liquidity coverage ratio (LCR) and the net stable funding ratio (NSFR).

- The LCR will require banks to have sufficient high quality liquid assets to withstand a 30 day stressed funding scenario that is specified by the regulators.

- The NSFR is a longer term structural ratio designed to address liquidity mismatches. It covers the entire balance sheet and provides incentives for banks to use stable sources of funding.

Furthermore Basel III is addressing derivatives and securities and increasing the capital charges for all organisations involved in those markets.

Not surprisingly, stress testing rules also featured. Under Basel III banks must have a comprehensive stress testing programme for counterparty risk which enables:

- Trade capture and exposure aggregation of all counterparties
- Regular stress testing of market risk factors
- Stress testing to be performed at least on a monthly basis
- A reduction of exposure to concentrations of directional sensitivities.

Wrong way risk arises when default risk and credit exposure increase together. Ordinarily in trading book credit risk measurement, the creditworthiness of the counterparty and the exposure of a transaction are measured and modelled independently. In a transaction where wrong-way risk may occur, this approach is simply not sufficient and ignores a significant source of potential loss.

Basel III addresses this phenomenon and requires that banks should identify exposures which generate wrong way risk. This can be done by stress testing and scenario planning in order to identify any possibility of severe shocks. Should risk factor relationships change, banks may well be affected. Hence, Basel III states that banks should monitor by product, industry, and region as relevant to their business. Regular reporting to board and risk committees about incidences and mitigation steps must be performed.

The Basel Accords are also concerned with operational risk. Basel defines seven categories of loss events. They are:

1   Internal fraud
2   External fraud
3   Employee practices and workplace safety
4   Clients, products and business practice
5   Damage to physical assets
6   Business disruption and system failures
7   Execution, delivery and process management.

Basel also maintains an operational loss database, which follows certain business lines and analyses losses accordingly. These are the main areas where substantial losses are anticipated. These lines include:

1   Corporate finance
2   Trading and sales
3   Retail banking
4   Commercial banking

5   Payments and settlement
6   Agency services
7   Asset management
8   Retail brokerage

These reviews deliver hard data showing the frequency by risk type and also across different business lines. The highest numbers of risk events have been proved to occur amongst external fraud, execution and delivery; and processes.

Answer 2

Traditional approaches to quality were focused on inspection. Modern approaches to quality focus on the prevention of defects through quality standards and processes.

In the past, quality control meant inspection. Inspection was usually carried out at three main points:

1   Receiving inspection
2   Floor or process inspection
3   Final inspection or testing.

The problem with this inspection approach is that it allows for and often entails built-in waste.

- The inspection process itself does not add value. If it could be guaranteed that no defective items were produced there would be no need for a separate inspection function.

- The inspection function itself requires resources, in both people and facilities.

- The production of substandard products is a waste of materials, machine time, human efforts, and overheads.

- The production of defects is not compatible with newer production techniques such as just-in-time where there is no time for inspection.

- Working capital is tied up in inventory (stocks).

- In the service industry, damage will have already been done to customer relations before inspection takes place.

Quality control involves establishing standards of quality for a product or service, sampling output by inspection or testing, taking appropriate corrective action and testing output to ensure reoccurrences are detected.

Quality management should aim to prevent defective production rather than simply detect it. Most modern approaches to quality have therefore tried to assure quality in the production process rather than inspecting goods or services after they have been produced.

The term quality assurance is used where a supplier guarantees the quality of goods or services they supply. Quality assurance programmes usually involve a close relationship between supplier and customer, which may extend to allowing customer representatives to view and/or monitor production procedures.

Quality assurance emphasises the processes and procedures used to produce a product or service; the logic being that if these are tightly controlled and monitored the resulting product and service will be high quality. As quality has been 'built-in', the need for inspection after production should be eliminated.

Answer 3

Regulation can be seen as an effort to protect various parties, as follows:

- To protect business entities, e.g. by enacting laws putting limits on market dominance by acting against monopolies and restrictive practices and by providing financial assistance to selected ailing industries and companies.

- To protect consumers through consumer protection regulations such as covering packaging, labelling, food hygiene and advertising.

- To protect employees with laws governing the recruitment of staff and health and safety legislation that regulates conditions of work.

- To protect third parties such as shareholders, suppliers and creditors through Companies Act regulation on capital maintenance and insolvency.

- To protect the interests of society at large against excessive business behaviour, e.g. by acting to protect the environment.

The financial services sector is vitally important to the UK economy, so it is essential that citizens and institutions remain confident in the ability of financial institutions to operate safely and efficiently. In an international context, it is also important to maintain the confidence of overseas investors.

The failure of large financial institutions presents 'systemic risks' that is, the stability of the financial system as a whole may be threatened. Financial services providers may become vulnerable at times of crisis, so there is an argument for there to be mechanisms in place that provide some form of safety net for firms.

The case may be made for having mechanisms in place to avoid the failure of banks and other firms that are 'too big to fail'. On the other hand, if financial institutions are aware that such mechanisms are in place, they may take greater risks, in the knowledge that they will be bailed out if failure threatens: this is known as the problem of moral hazard.

Following the global financial crisis, a new approach to financial regulation was required. In February 2013 the Financial Services (Banking Reform) Bill was introduced to Parliament. The Bill focused on changing the structure and delivery of regulation within the financial services sector.

After the financial crisis the FSA was criticised for providing what became known as 'too little, too late' regulation. A new regulatory regime was created and the FSA was replaced with a new regulatory structure comprising the:

- Bank of England
- Financial Policy Committee (FPC)
- Prudential Regulatory Authority (PRA)
- Financial Conduct Authority (FCA).

The Bank of England has responsibility to protect and enhance the stability of the financial system of the UK. In support of this objective, the Financial Policy Committee (FPC), which sits within the Bank of England, is charged with identifying, monitoring and acting to remove or reduce any risks which threaten the banking system in the UK. The FPC replaced the earlier Financial Stability Committee (FSC) set up within the BoE.

The FPC is able to make recommendations and give direction to the Prudential Regulation Authority (PRA) and the Financial Conduct Authority (FCA) on specific actions that should be taken in order to achieve this objective. It also has a secondary objective to support the economic policy of the Government.

Answer 4

Service quality is the totality of features and characteristics of that service which impacts on its ability to meet stated or implied needs.

Major factors that shape customer expectations include:

Marketing: claims may be difficult to deliver, e.g. an optician advertises that no appointments are required, but a client has to actually wait 50 minutes for an eye test.

Price: customer expectations usually increase as price increases, e.g. if a hair salon charges high prices, clients expect a good cut and styling.

Alternatives: a good past experience at one service provider is likely to set the standard next time for an alternative service provider.

Word of mouth: often this is the most influential source for setting up customer expectations.

Previous experience: this helps the customer develop a clearer view of what to expect. This adds to the challenge faced by the service provider but on the other hand also helps to moderate the consumers' expectations, e.g. experience of travelling with a certain rail service may inject a certain sense of reality into what a passenger can expect.

Customer's mood and attitude: it is inevitable that a customer's mood and attitude is likely to influence their expectations.

There are various ways in which service quality factors may be classified.

Hygiene factors: these are very much base line factors. If not present they will tend to dissatisfy a customer, e.g. a hotel guest will expect proper security but it is unlikely to delight.

Enhancing factors: these may partially delight but will not be a source of dissatisfaction if absent, e.g. a hotel guest is likely to really appreciate friendly staff but might not be dissatisfied if they are not all that cheerful.

Critical factors: these have the potential to delight as well as dissatisfy, e.g. a hotel guest will expect staff responsiveness.

Neutral factors: these usually have little impact on satisfaction, e.g. a hotel guest may be delighted if a hotel is aesthetically pleasing with nice wallpaper, smart fittings etc, but may well not miss them if not present.

Answer 5

Process maps aim to identify and represent the steps and decisions involved in a process, in diagrammatic form.

Process maps:

- Describe the flow of materials, information and documents
- Display the tasks contained within the process
- Show that the tasks transform inputs into outputs
- Indicate the decisions that need to be made
- Demonstrate the relationships and dependencies between the process steps

There are many types of process maps (also known as process charts) and many charting conventions. Two common types of process map are:

- A 'basic' flowchart which provides a basic 'birds eye' view

- A deployment chart which provides an overview and also indicates where or by whom actions are performed.

Process maps should be simple enough for the process under review to be understood by almost anyone, even someone unfamiliar with the process.

Process maps are important for several reasons.

- Changing systems and working methods without understanding the underlying processes can lead to costly mistakes. It can also create conditions that make it difficult for staff to work effectively.

- If organisations don't understand a process they will not be able to manage it effectively and if they cannot manage a process they cannot improve it.

- Process mapping enables businesses to clearly define current processes, identifying problem areas such as bottlenecks, delays or waste. This knowledge provides a solid basis from which to develop solutions and plan new improved processes.

- Process mapping enables an organisation to:

    - Establish what is currently happening and why

    - Measure how efficiently the process is working

    - Gather information to understand where waste and inefficiencies exist and their impact on employees, customers and/or partners

    - Develop new, improved processes to reduce or eliminate inefficiency.

The benefits of process mapping include:

- Identifies opportunities to standardise and simplify processes

- Identifies areas of inefficiency and waste such as duplication of effort

- Identifies potential bottlenecks or pinch points (which could lead to delays and any inefficiencies resulting from those delays)

- Provides management with an overall understanding of how the processes under their control operate

- Allows workers to better understand their role and how their work fits into the organisation's operations

- Provides support to new initiatives such as lean production and customer satisfaction improvements.

PRACTICE EXAMINATION 4

Question 1 *Chapter 14*

Organisations, and futurists, often need to collect information concerning external, environmental factors. These factors are outside of the control of the business, but can have a significant impact on it. A useful mnemonic that strategists and futurologists consider is STEEP.

Required

(a)   What does STEEP stand for?   **(1 mark)**
(b)   Provide examples for each constituent part of the mnemonic.   **(4 marks)**
(c)   Use STEEP to analyse the threats and opportunities of the airline industry.   **(25 marks)**
(d)   Summarise how attractive the airline industry is, and how air travel may change in the future.

                                                                                                             (10 marks)

                                                                                                             (Total 40 marks)

Question 2

Required

What is the role of a Risk Committee and what key responsibilities do they have?   **(15 marks)**

                                                                                                             (Total 15 marks)

Question 3

Required   *Chapter 12*

(a)   What is 'Big Data'?   **(5 marks)**
(b)   What are the benefits of Big Data analytics and what challenges does it bring?   **(10 marks)**

                                                                                                             (Total 15 marks)

Question 4 *Chapter 7*

There are a number of supply and sourcing strategies used by businesses.

Single, multiple, Delegated, Parallel

Required

(a)   Describe the different types of sourcing strategies.   **(5 marks)**
(b)   Outline the advantages and disadvantages of each one.   **(10 marks)**

                                                                                                             (Total 15 marks)

Question 5 *Chapter 4*

Corporate social responsibility is a form of corporate self-regulation integrated into a business model.

Required

(a)   What is the distinction between corporate social responsibility and ethics?   **(5 marks)**
(b)   What are the arguments in favour and arguments against CSR?   **(10 marks)**

                                                                                                             (Total 15 marks)

PRACTICE EXAMINATION 4
ANSWERS

Answer 1

STEEP stands for:

Society/social
Technology
Economic
Environmental
Political/legal

Society/social

Population changes/demographics, social mobility and disposable income levels can all impact. Changes in society's views may put pressure on how the organisation is run, for example pressure to reduce environmental pollution. Corporate social responsibility and sustainability play an important role here.

Technology

- Technological advances may affect an organisation's production and/or management processes.
- Technology may also allow the development of new products and services which were not previously possible.

Environmental

Pollution and wastage that have social or legal consequences, such as greenhouse emissions, carbon footprint, changing attitudes to recycling, will all impact.

Economic

Economic factors affect an organisation's finances such as the availability of finance or sales levels. In addition, interest rates, exchange rates, tax rates and inflation will impact. Economic stability or instability will affect investors/consumers confidence.

Political/legal

National or local politics may affect how an organisation operates. Political stability or instability will impact positively or negatively. Changes in legislation may put new responsibilities or liabilities on an organisation. For example, local authorities providing help and support to local businesses in order to increase employment in their area.

The airline industry

Social factors

- Passenger numbers continue to increase despite the economic slowdown; business travel is more sustainable than leisure travel.

- Business travellers are important to airlines because they are more likely to travel several times throughout the year and they tend to purchase upgraded services that have higher margins for the airline.

- Leisure travellers are less likely to purchase premium services and are typically very price sensitive. In times of economic uncertainty or a sharp decline in consumer confidence, the number of leisure travellers is expected to decline.

- There has been a move to no-frills cheap services for short haul flights.

- Customer service is critical. Strikes by check-in staff and cabin crews can impact market share.

Technological factors

- Ticketless travel is more commonplace and this will grow, thereby reducing the costs of travel agents' commissions.

- Super-sized carriers are now in production, with some aircraft able to carry 800+ travellers.

- Video conferencing and the internet may pose a threat to business travel; however, this threat is yet to emerge.

Environmental factors

- Weather is variable and unpredictable. Extreme heat, cold, fog and snow can shut down airports and cancel flights, as can natural disasters such as the volcanic eruption in Iceland in 2010. This increases costs for the airlines and airports.

- Noise and pollution.

- Carbon emissions.

Economic factors

The three largest costs for airlines are: labour; fuel; and borrowing/financing costs.

- Labour costs are an airline's biggest cost as they must pay pilots, flight attendants, baggage handlers, dispatchers and other customer service staff.

- Fuel makes up a significant portion of an airline's total costs, although efficiency among different carriers can vary widely. Short haul airlines typically get lower fuel efficiency because take-offs and landings consume high amounts of jet fuel. Fuel costs vary considerably due to supply and demand and are expected to increase in recessionary periods as demand falls.

- Recent lower worldwide interest rates have led to lower operating lease costs and airlines are taking advantage of cheaper financing deals.

- Passengers are becoming increasingly reluctant to pay more for flights. The largest proportion of an airlines' revenue is derived from regular and business passengers. The pressure to reduce costs and switching from business class to economy is expected to continue. Business confidence is an important factor.

Political factors

- Government protection of national airlines is still prevalent in many countries and this is expected to continue.

- In Europe, government subsidies for airlines will eventually come to an end.

- The impact of terrorism and continued conflict in the Middle East.

- Deregulation.

- Planning permission is becoming increasingly important as slots become critical factors, e.g. Terminal 5 at Heathrow and the proposed new airport in London.

- Increased pressure from the noise abatement lobbies.

- Increased difficulty in opening new airports or extending existing runways.

Summary

Overall, the airline industry is becoming less attractive than it was. Growth is stagnant because of terrorism and the global economic slowdown. Low-cost carriers are squeezing established players in the industry. Buyers are able to shop around and business users are moving to economy class or low-cost providers. Costs continue to increase, which will impact negatively on the industry's future earning power.

The future

As competition for energy resources intensify increasing the cost of fuel and air travel will force airline operators to look at alternative, greener ways of powering their machines such as bio fuels.

Technological advances will eliminate the need for check-in lines and desks.

Luggage tags of the future will use technology that allows you to trace your suitcase's whereabouts at all times. This could integrate with a computerised baggage handling system.

Biometric face recognition software and machine-readable passports incorporating a digital boarding pass will mean that clearing customs will take less time, and high-speed laser molecular scanners will security check hand luggage in seconds.

Computers, through analysing our searches online and cross-referencing our preferences, will be able to use predictive algorithms to make tailored suggestions. This predictive software will also likely take into consideration the personal data we post about ourselves on social media when developing detailed itineraries.

Breakthroughs in medicine, which will see people living longer and remaining active much later into life. As the baby boom generation start retiring, they will not want to settle down so expect to see more people in their 60s and 70s looking for adventure and requesting more skiing or trekking type holidays.

There could also be a sharp rise in learning tourism where groups travel to destinations and incorporate sightseeing with informative talks and seminars.

Answer 2

Not all companies will have a Risk Committee, because the function can be performed by the audit committee. However, they are common in banks due to the nature of the business. If there is no Risk Committee, the responsibilities it would have are usually fulfilled by the audit committee.

In line with best practice and the recommendation of the Walker Report, the Risk Committee should be chaired by a non-executive director and have as a member of its group the Chief Risk Officer (CRO) acting for the bank.

The CRO is the executive accountable for enabling the efficient and effective governance of significant risks and related opportunities to a business and its various segments. CROs are accountable to the Executive Committee and the Board for enabling the business to balance risk and reward.

In more complex organisations, they are generally responsible for co-ordinating the organisation's Enterprise Wide Risk Management (EWRM) approach.

The committee should have the power to oversee, and prevent if appropriate, large-scale transactions.

The Risk Committee is responsible for designing, implementing and reviewing risk management strategies and will comprise of a mixture of executive and non-executive directors.

Key responsibilities of a Risk Committee include:

- Approval of risk management strategy

- Ensuring compliance with legal and other requirements directly relating to risk, such as legislation on credit, employment law and health and safety issues

- Reporting to the board and to shareholders

- Focusing on financial risks so that high level liaison with external auditors can be more effective

- Formulating policy responses to risk, based on senior executive input and internal/external information

- Consideration of reports on matters relevant to risk management

- Evaluating the effectiveness of risk management and systems, and driving necessary changes

- Monitoring risk exposures in key areas

- Troubleshooting matters that require senior level attention

- Liaising with the Audit Committee on internal controls.

Answer 3

Big Data is a popular term used to describe the exponential growth and availability of data, both structured and unstructured. Big Data may be as important to business and society as the internet has become.

In a commercial setting 'Big Data' is being used to identify trends that may exist in vast quantities of data in the pursuit of value creation. Historically, organisations have been restricted as to the amount of data that they can process due to the storage limitations of existing computer systems.

Big Data management is a term relating to the storage and administration of large volumes of data in all forms. Once stored, Big Data analytics are used to analyse the data to identify relationships, patterns and other correlations in order to develop corporate strategy to improve profitability.

Due to the emergence of 'cloud based' data storage providers and improved computer technologies, these problems are gradually being overcome.

There are a number of potential benefits to organisations undertaking big data analytics.

- **Examine vast quantities of data relatively quickly**: Big Data analytics allows for large quantities of data to be examined to identify trends and correlations eg shopper buying habits.

- **Improves organisational decision making**: better data analysis help management to take advantage of current social trends by introducing new products to meet customer's needs.

- **Greater focus on the individual customer**: organisations can target special offers or discounts directly to individual customers to entice repeat business.

- **Cost reduction**: improved data about customers and internal operations may help to reduce costs.

A significant number of large entities have already turned to 'Big Data analytics' with the aim of gaining a competitive advantage over their rivals. Proponents of 'Big Data analytics' argue that the insights gained may lead to improvements throughout the entire organisation.

The challenge for big business has been to capture and analyse these vast quantities of data which may be of use in a commercial context. Data is only as good as the intelligence gleaned from it, and that entails effective data analytics and a whole lot of computing power to cope with the exponential increase in volume.

It should also be noted that the rise of 'Big Data' has had its implications. Organisations looking to exploit the opportunities presented have encountered a significant shortage of individuals with the required skills in the job market to analyse the data.

Questions have also been raised over who ultimately owns the data that organisations hold and who is responsible for keeping such data safe from hackers. Does it belong to the individual or customer, the company, the service provider hosting the data or the national jurisdiction the where the data is held?

Answer 4

Organisations may use a number of suppliers for their raw materials, and there are a range of possible strategies open to an organisation when deciding who they will purchase their supplies from.
For example:

- Certain suppliers may produce a better quality of product.

- Some suppliers may be cheaper on price.

- Suppliers may also be selected from a number of countries to guard against the risk of supplies from one country being affected by circumstances such as war, trade barriers, bad weather etc.

- Suppliers are of different sizes so buyers can match order sizes to appropriate suppliers (i.e. small suppliers may not be suitable for larger orders).

- Expertise varies between suppliers so building relationships with a number of them can help the buyer make more informed choices.

The mix of suppliers should be optimised so that the organisation maximises the benefits they offer and minimises any risks involved in supply.

The following strategies may be followed when deciding on a supply strategy:

Single: the buyer chooses one source of supply.

Advantages

- Stronger relationships with the supplier

- Possible source of superior quality due to increased opportunity for a supplier quality assurance programme

- Facilitates better communication

- Economies of scale

- Facilitates confidentiality

- Possible source of competitive advantage

Disadvantages

- Vulnerable to any disruption in supply
- The buyer is dependent on the supplier
- Supplier power may increase if no alternative supplier exists
- The supplier is vulnerable to shifts in order levels

Multiple: the buyer chooses several sources of supply

Advantages

- Access to a wide range of knowledge and expertise

- Competition among suppliers may drive the price down

- Supply failure by one supplier will cause minimal disruption, if it is easy to switch between suppliers

Disadvantages

- Not easy to develop an effective quality assurance programme
- Suppliers may display less commitment
- Economies of scale are neglected

Delegated: a supplier is given responsibility for the delivery of a complete sub-assembly. For example, rather than dealing with several suppliers a 'first-tier' supplier would be appointed to deliver a complete sub-assembly (e.g. a PC manufacturer may delegate the production of keyboards).

Advantages

- Allows the utilisation of specialist external expertise
- Frees-up internal staff for other tasks
- The purchasing entity may be able to negotiate economies of scale

Disadvantages

- Quality control is difficult to maintain

- Loss of confidentiality if products use trade secrets

- Competitors may utilise the same external organisation so it is unlikely to be a source of competitive advantage

Parallel: parallel sourcing involves mixing/combining the other three approaches to maximise the benefits of each

Advantages

- If used correctly should provide an efficient/effective strategy
- Supplier failure will not halt production
- Price competition is created between suppliers

Disadvantages

- Can be complicated to manage
- Quality control is difficult to maintain

Answer 5

CSR policy functions as a built-in, self-regulating mechanism whereby a business monitors and ensures its active compliance with the spirit of the law, ethical standards and international norms. It is a process that aims to embrace responsibility for the company's actions and, through its activities, encourage a positive impact on the environment, consumers, employees, communities and other stakeholders.

CSR and business ethics are similar in that both are concerned with values, objectives and decisions based on something other than just the pursuit of profit.

The two concepts are closely linked:

1   A socially responsible firm should be an ethical firm.
2   An ethical firm should be socially responsible.

However, there is also a distinction between the two:

- CSR is about responsibility to all stakeholders and not just shareholders.
- Ethics is about morally correct behaviour.

Some people equate moral behaviour with legal behaviour, disregarding the fact that even though an action may not be illegal, it still may not be moral. Yet some contend that the only requirement is to obey the law. They ignore the spirit of the law by only following the letter of the law.

Arguments in favour of CSR

Consumer expectations

There is an increasing expectation from consumers and other stakeholders that businesses will act in a more socially responsible manner. Consumers are becoming more aware of the origins of the everyday things they buy, and they want to buy products that are responsibly sourced. Given that one of the key success factors for a business is the ability to offer customers what they want, then offering products and services which are deemed to be socially responsible should help boost sales. CSR could also provide opportunities to enter new markets or develop new products.

Brand name

Being seen as socially responsible can help enhance a business's reputation and therefore its brand. Customers may prefer to deal with a business they feel is socially responsible rather than with one which is not. Therefore, CSR could actually be a source of differentiation for a business.

Lower environmental costs

If organisations improve the efficiency of their energy usage then as well as making lower emissions they will also have lower cost bases. If they can achieve a lower cost base through the efficient use of resources, this could help them create (or improve) their competitive advantage. More generally, organisations could also find it is less costly to regulate their own activities voluntarily than ignoring socially responsibility in the short term and then having to comply with statutory regulations (in the form of taxes or fines, for example) which may be imposed on them later.

Trading partnerships

If organisations are perceived as not being socially responsible, they may find it harder to attract trading partners, or support from nations and local communities where they might want to invest.

Access to staff

The way organisations are perceived to treat their staff may affect their ability to attract staff. For example, if they are perceived to offer good working conditions are more likely to be able to attract a higher calibre of staff than competitors who are perceived to offer unfavourable working conditions. In turn, an organisation which is able to attract (and retain) high quality staff may be able to generate competitive advantage over a competitor which is less able to attract good quality staff.

Investment and funding

An organisation's reputation may also affect its ability to attract finance, particularly from ethical investors. For example, obtaining a listing on the FTSE4Good (index of companies that meet globally recognised corporate responsibility standards) is likely to help them attract finance from ethical investors.

Sustainable business

Taken collectively, the arguments in favour of CSR suggest that a socially responsible business is likely to be able to operate for longer in society than a less responsible one. In turn, if the business can expect more years of cash flows in the future, it might be reasonable to expect the value of the company to be higher than that of one whose future is perceived to be less secure.

Arguments against corporate social responsibility

Some commentators have argued against corporate social responsibility along the following lines:

Businesses do not have responsibilities, only people have responsibilities. Managers in charge of organisations are responsible to the owners of the business, by whom they are employed.

Some people argue that the social responsibility model is politically collectivist in nature. This is the idea that people should prioritise the good of society over the welfare of the individual and so CSR should not be extended any further than absolutely necessary in a free society. They argue that the maximisation of wealth is the best way that society can benefit from a business's activities because:

- Maximising wealth has the effect of increasing the tax revenues available to the state to disburse on socially desirable objectives.

- Maximising shareholder value has a 'trickle down' effect on other disadvantaged members of society.